WORD TRANSLATIONS

Math Preparation Guide

This comprehensive guide analyzes the GMAT's complex word problems and provides structured frameworks for attacking each question type. Master the art of translating challenging word problems into organized data.

Word Translations GMAT Preparation Guide, 2007 Edition

10-digit International Standard Book Number: 0-9790175-3-X
13-digit International Standard Book Number: 978-0-9790175-3-7

Note: *GMAT, Graduate Management Admission Test, Graduate Management Admission Council,* and *GMAC* are all registered trademarks of the Graduate Management Admission Council which neither sponsors nor is affiliated in any way with this product.

8 GUIDE INSTRUCTIONAL SERIES

Math GMAT Preparation Guides

Number Properties (ISBN: 978-0-9790175-0-6)

Fractions, Decimals, & Percents (ISBN: 978-0-9790175-1-3)

Equations, Inequalities, & VIC's (ISBN: 978-0-9790175-2-0)

Word Translations (ISBN: 978-0-9790175-3-7)

Geometry (ISBN: 978-0-9790175-4-4)

Verbal GMAT Preparation Guides

Critical Reasoning (ISBN: 978-0-9790175-5-1)

Reading Comprehension (ISBN: 978-0-9790175 6 8)

Sentence Correction (ISBN: 978-0-9790175-7-5)

HOW OUR GMAT PREP BOOKS ARE DIFFERENT

One of our core beliefs at Manhattan GMAT is that a curriculum should be more than just a guidebook of tricks and tips. Scoring well on the GMAT requires a curriculum that builds true content knowledge and understanding. Skim through this guide and this is what you will see:

You will *not* find page after page of guessing techniques.

Instead, you will find a highly organized and structured guide that actually teaches you the content you need to know to do well on the GMAT.

You *will* find many more pages-per-topic than in all-in-one tomes.

Each chapter covers one specific topic area in-depth, explaining key concepts, detailing in-depth strategies, and building specific skills through Manhattan GMAT's *In-Action* problem sets (with comprehensive explanations). Why are there 8 guides? Each of the 8 books (5 Math, 3 Verbal) covers a major content area in extensive depth, allowing you to delve into each topic in great detail. In addition, you may purchase only those guides that pertain to those areas in which you need to improve.

This guide is challenging - it asks you to do more, not less.

It starts with the fundamental skills, but does not end there; it also includes the *most advanced content* that many other prep books ignore. As the average GMAT score required to gain admission to top business schools continues to rise, this guide, together with the 6 computer adaptive online practice exams and bonus question bank included with your purchase, provides test-takers with the depth and volume of advanced material essential for achieving the highest scores, given the GMAT's computer adaptive format.

This guide is ambitious - developing mastery is its goal.

Developed by Manhattan GMAT's staff of REAL teachers (all of whom have 99th percentile official GMAT scores), our ambitious curriculum seeks to provide test-takers of all levels with an in-depth and carefully tailored approach that enables our students to achieve mastery. If you are looking to learn more than just the "process of elimination" and if you want to develop skills, strategies, and a confident approach to any problem that you may see on the GMAT, then our sophisticated preparation guides are the tools to get you there.

HOW TO ACCESS YOUR ONLINE RESOURCES

Please read this entire page of information, all the way down to the bottom of the page! This page describes WHAT online resources are included with the purchase of this book and HOW to access these resources.

[**If you are a registered Manhattan GMAT student** and have received this book as part of your course materials, you have AUTOMATIC access to ALL of our online resources. This includes all simulated practice exams, question banks, and online updates to this book. To access these resources, follow the instructions in the Welcome Guide provided to you at the start of your program. Do NOT follow the instructions below.]

If you have purchased this book, your purchase includes 1 YEAR OF ONLINE ACCESS to the following:

> **6 Computer Adaptive Online Practice Exams**

> **Bonus Online Question Bank for WORD TRANSLATIONS**

> **Online Updates to the Content in this Book**

The 6 full-length computer adaptive practice exams included with the purchase of this book are delivered online using Manhattan GMAT's proprietary computer adaptive online test engine. The exams adapt to your ability level by drawing from a bank of more than 1200 unique questions of varying difficulty levels written by Manhattan GMAT's expert instructors, all of whom have scored in the 99th percentile on the Official GMAT. At the end of each exam you will receive a score, an analysis of your results, and the opportunity to review detailed explanations for each question. You may choose to take the exams timed or untimed.

The Bonus Online Question Bank for Word Translations consists of 25 extra practice questions (with detailed explanations) that test the variety of Word Translation concepts and skills covered in this book. These questions provide you with extra practice *beyond* the problem sets contained in this book. You may use our online timer to practice your pacing by setting time limits for each question in the bank.

The content presented in this book is updated periodically to ensure that it reflects the GMAT's most current trends. You may view all updates, including any known errors or changes, upon registering for online access.

Important Note: The 6 computer adaptive online exams included with the purchase of this book are the SAME exams that you receive upon purchasing ANY book in Manhattan GMAT's 8 Book Preparation Series. On the other hand, the Bonus Online Question Bank for WORD TRANSLATIONS is a unique resource that you receive ONLY with the purchase of this specific title.

> To access the online resources listed above, you will need this book in front of you and you will need to register your information online. This book includes access to the above resources for ONE PERSON ONLY.
>
> *To register and start using your online resources, please go online to the following URL:*
>
> **http://www.manhattangmat.com/access.cfm**   (Double check that you have typed this in accurately!)
>
> Your one-year of online access begins on the day that you register at the above URL. You only need to register your product ONCE at the above URL. To use your online resources any time AFTER you have completed the registration process, please login to the following URL:
>
> **http://www.manhattangmat.com/practicecenter.cfm**

TABLE OF CONTENTS

g

Chapter 1
of

WORD TRANSLATIONS

ALGEBRAIC
TRANSLATIONS

In This Chapter . . .

- Algebraic Translations
- Using Charts to Organize Variables
- Age Charts

Algebraic Translations

To solve many word problems on the GMAT, you must be able to translate English into algebra. To do this, select variables and variable expressions to represent unknown quantities, and then write equations to state relations between the unknowns and the known values. Once you have written one or more algebraic equations to represent a problem, you can solve them to find any missing information.

> **A candy company offers premium chocolates at $5 per pound. They also offer regular chocolates at $4 per pound. If Barrett buys Michelle a 7-pound box of Valentines chocolates that costs him $31, how many pounds of premium chocolates are in the box?**

To solve this problem, simply translate the words into algebraic equations:

Be sure to make a note of what each variable represents.

Step 1: Assign variables.

If possible, use only one variable to represent the unknown information. If there are two unknown quantities, you will often be able to use relationships in the problem to write an expression for a second unknown in terms of the same variable you used for the first unknown.

Let p = the number of pounds of premium chocolate
Let $7 - p$ = the number of pounds of regular chocolate

Step 2: Write equation(s).

If you are not sure how to construct the equation, begin by expressing a relationship between the unknowns and the known values in words. For example, in this problem, you might say:

"The total cost of the box is equal to the cost of the premium chocolates plus the cost of the regular chocolates."

Then, translate the relationship you have written into mathematical symbols:

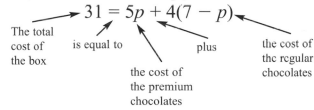

$$31 = 5p + 4(7 - p)$$

The total cost of the box — is equal to — the cost of the premium chocolates — plus — the cost of the regular chocolates

Step 3: Solve.

$$31 = 5p + 4(7 - p)$$
$$31 = 5p + 28 - 4p$$
$$3 = p$$

Step 4: Evaluate the algebraic solution in the context of the problem.

Once you solve for the unknown, look back at the problem and make sure you answer the question asked. In this problem, we are asked for the number of pounds of premium chocolate in the box. Notice that we wisely chose our unknown variable p to represent the number of pounds of premium chocolate, so that, once we solved for p, there would be no additional steps to take.

Using Charts to Organize Variables

When an algebraic translation problem involves several variables with multiple relation-ships, it is often a good idea to make a chart to organize information.

One type of algebraic translation that appears on the GMAT is the age problem type. Age problems are those that ask you to find the age of an individual at a certain point in time, given some information about other people's ages, at other times.

Complicated age problems are most effectively solved using an AGE CHART. Consider the following example:

> **8 years ago, George was half as old as Sarah. Sarah is now 20 years older than George. How old will George be 10 years from now?**

The age chart doesn't relate the ages of the individuals. It simply helps you to assign variables you can use to write equations.

Step 1: Assign Variables.
Use an age chart to help you keep track of the variables in this problem.

	8 years ago	Now	10 years from now
George	$G - 8$	G	$G + 10$
Sarah	$S - 8$	S	$S + 10$

Step 2: Write equation(s).
Using the information in the problem, write equations that relate the individuals' ages together.

According to this problem, 8 years ago, George was half as old as Sarah. Using the age expressions from the "8 years ago" column, we can write the following equation:

$$G - 8 = \frac{S - 8}{2} \qquad \text{which can be rewritten} \qquad 2G - 16 = S - 8$$

According to this problem, Sarah is 20 years older than George. Using the age expressions from the "Now" column, we can write the following equation: $G + 20 = S$.

Step 3: Solve.
In this problem we can subtract the second equation from the first.

$$
\begin{aligned}
2G - 16 &= S - 8 \\
-\ (G + 20 &= S) \\
\hline
G - 36 &= -8 \\
G &= 28
\end{aligned}
$$

Step 4: Evaluate the algebraic solution in the context of the problem.
In this problem, we are asked to find George's age in 10 years. Since George is now 28 years old, he will be 38 in 10 years.

Problem Set

Solve the following problems with the four-step method outlined in this section.

1. John is 20 years older than Brian. 12 years ago, John was twice as old as Brian. How old is Brian?

2. Mrs. Smythe has two dogs, Jackie and Stella, who weigh a total of 75 pounds. If Stella weighs 15 pounds less than twice Jackie's weight, how much does Stella weigh?

3. Caleb spends $72.50 on 50 hamburgers for the marching band. If single burgers cost $1.00 each and double burgers cost $1.50 each, how many double burgers did he buy?

4. Abigail is 4 times older than Bonnie. In 6 years, Bonnie will be twice as old as Candice. If, 4 years from now, Abigail will be 36 years old, how old will Candice be in 6 years?

5. United Telephone charges a base rate of $10.00 for service, plus an additional charge of $0.25 per minute. Atlantic Call charges a base rate of $12.00 for service, plus an additional charge of $0.20 per minute. For what number of minutes would the bills for each telephone company be the same?

6. Ross is 3 times as old as Sam, and Sam is 3 years older than Tina. 2 years from now, Tina will drink from the Fountain of Youth, which will make her half as old as she was. If after drinking from the Fountain, Tina is 16 years old, how old is Ross right now?

7. Carina has 100 ounces of coffee divided into 5- and 10-ounce packages. If she has 2 more 5-ounce packages than 10-ounce packages, how many 10-ounce packages does she have?

8. Carla cuts a 70-inch piece of ribbon into 2 pieces. If the first piece is five inches more than one fourth as long as the second piece, how long is the longer piece of ribbon?

9. In a used car lot, there are 3 times as many red cars as green cars. If tomorrow 12 green cars are sold and 3 red cars are added, then there will be 6 times as many red cars as green cars. How many green cars are currently in the lot?

10. Jane started baby-sitting when she was 18 years old. However, she only baby-sat children who were, at most, half her age. Jane is currently 32 years old, and she stopped baby-sitting 10 years ago. What is the current age of the oldest person that Jane could have baby-sat?

11. If Tessie triples her money at blackjack and then leaves a ten-dollar tip for the dealer, she will leave the casino with the same amount of money as if she had won 190 dollars at roulette. How much money did Tessie take into the casino?

12. Mehmet buys 3 pencils, 2 notebooks, and an eraser for 80 cents. At the same store, Gloria buys 5 pencils, 5 notebooks, and an eraser for $1.45. Stan buys a pencil, a notebook, and an eraser for 45 cents. What is the price of each item?

13. Andrew will be half as old as Larry in 3 years. Andrew will also be one-third as old as Jerome in 5 years. If Jerome is 15 years older than Larry, how old is Andrew?

14. A circus earned $150,000 in ticket revenue by selling 1,800 V.I.P. and Standard tickets. They sold 25% more Standard tickets than V.I.P. tickets. If the revenue from Standard tickets represents a third of the total ticket revenue, what is the price of a V.I.P. ticket?

15. 8 years from now, the bottle of wine labeled 'Aged' will be 7 times older than the bottle of wine labeled 'Table.' 1 year ago, the bottle of wine labeled 'Table' was one-fourth as old as the bottle of wine labeled 'Vintage.' If the 'Aged' bottle was 20 times older than the 'Vintage' bottle 2 years ago, then how old is each bottle now?

1. **32:** Use an age chart to assign variables. Then write equations, using the information given in the problem:

	12 years ago	Now
John	$j - 12$	j
Brian	$b - 12$	b

John is 20 years older than Brian:
$$j = b + 20$$

12 years ago, John was twice as old as Brian:
$$(j - 12) = 2(b - 12)$$
$$j - 12 = 2b - 24$$
$$j = 2b - 12$$

Combine the two equations by setting the two values for j equal to each other:
$$b + 20 = 2b - 12$$
$$b = 32$$

2. **45 pounds:**

Let j = Jackie's weight
Let s = Stella's weight

The two dogs weigh a total of 75 pounds:
$$j + s = 75$$

Stella weighs 15 pounds less than twice Jackie's weight:
$$s = 2j - 15$$

Combine the two equations by substituting the value for s from equation (2) into equation (1).
$$j + (2j - 15) = 75$$
$$3j - 15 = 75$$
$$3j = 90$$
$$j = 30$$

Find Stella's weight by substituting Jackie's weight into equation (1).
$$30 + s = 75$$
$$s = 45$$

3. **45 double burgers:**

Let s = the number of single burgers purchased
Let d = the number of double burgers purchased

Caleb bought 50 burgers:
$$s + d = 50$$

Caleb spent \$72.50 in all:
$$s + 1.5d = 72.50$$

Combine the two equations by subtracting equation (1) from equation (2).
$$s + 1.5d = 72.50$$
$$\underline{- s + d = 50}$$
$$.5d = 22.5$$
$$d = 45$$

4. **7:** Use an age chart to assign variables. Then write equations, using the information given in the problem:

	Now	in 4 years	in 6 years
Abigail	a	$a + 4$	$a + 6$
Bonnie	b	$b + 4$	$b + 6$
Candice	c	$c + 4$	$c + 6$

Abigail is 4 times older than Bonnie:
$$a = 4b$$

In 6 years, Bonnie will be twice as old as Candice:
$$b + 6 = 2(c + 6)$$

4 years from now, Abigail will be 36 years old:
$$a + 4 = 36$$

First, solve the single-variable equation (equation 3) to find the value of a:
$$a + 4 = 36$$
$$a = 32$$
Then, substitute this value into equation (1) to find the value of b:
$$32 = 4b$$
$$b = 8$$
Substitute this value into equation (2) to find the value of c:
$$8 + 6 = 2(c + 6)$$
$$14 = 2c + 12$$
$$2c = 2$$
$$c = 1$$
If Candice is 1 year old now, then in 6 years she will be 7 years old.

5. **40 minutes:**
Let x = the number of minutes
A call made by United Telephone costs \$10.00 plus \$0.25 per minute: $10 + .25x$.
A call made by Atlantic Call costs \$12.00 plus \$0.20 per minute: $12 + .20x$.

Set the expressions equal to each other:
$$10 + .25x = 12 + .20x$$
$$.05x = 2$$
$$x = 40$$

6. **99:** Use an age chart to assign variables. Then write equations, using the information given in the problem:

	Now	in 2 years
Ross	r	$r + 2$
Sam	s	$s + 2$
Tina	t	$t + 2$

Ross is 3 times as old as Sam: $r = 3s$.
Sam is 3 years older than Tina: $s = t + 3$.

In 2 years, Tina will be 16 (half as old as she was): $\dfrac{t + 2}{2} = 16$.

Work backwards to solve the problem:

$t + 2 = 32$	$s = 30 + 3$	$r = 3(33)$
$t = 30$	$s = 33$	$r = 99$

7. **6:**

　　　Let a = the number of 5-ounce packages
　　　Let b = the number of 10-ounce packages

Carina has 100 ounces of coffee:　　She has two more 5-ounce packages than 10-ounce packages:
　　$5a + 10b = 100$　　　　　　　　$a = b + 2$

Combine the equations by substituting the value of a from equation (2) into equation (1).
　　　$5(b + 2) + 10b = 100$
　　　$5b + 10 + 10b = 100$
　　　　$15b + 10 = 100$
　　　　　$15b = 90$
　　　　　　$b = 6$

8. **52 inches:**

　　　Let x = the 1st piece of ribbon
　　　Let y = the 2nd piece of ribbon

The ribbon is 70 inches long:　　The 1st piece is 5 inches more than 1/4 as long as the 2nd:

　　$x + y = 70$　　　　　　　　　$x = 5 + \dfrac{y}{4}$

Combine the equations by substituting the value of x from equation (2) into equation (1):

　　$5 + \dfrac{y}{4} + y = 70$

　　$20 + y + 4y = 280$
　　　　　$5y = 260$
　　　　　　$y = 52$

9. **25:**

　　　Let g = the number of green cars
　　　Let r = the number of red cars

There are 3 times as many red cars as　　If 12 green cars are sold and 3 red cars are added,
green cars:　　　　　　　　　　　there will be 6 times as many red cars as green ones:
　　$r = 3g$　　　　　　　　　　　$3 + r = 6(g - 12)$

Combine the equations by substituting the value of r from equation (1) into equation (2):
　　$3 + 3g = 6g - 72$
　　　　$3g = 75$
　　　　　$g = 25$

10. **23:** Since you are given actual ages for Jane, the easiest way to solve the problem is to think about the extreme scenarios. At one extreme, 18 year-old Jane could have baby-sat a child of age 9. Since Jane is now 32, that child would now be 23. At the other extreme, 22 year-old Jane could have baby-sat a child of age 11. Since Jane is now 32 that child would now be 21. We can see that the first scenario yields the oldest possible current age (23) of a child that Jane baby-sat.

11. **$100:**

Let x = the amount of money Tessie took into the casino

If Tessie triples her money and then leaves a ten-dollar tip, she will have $3x - 10$ dollars left. If she had won 190 dollars, she would have had $x + 190$ dollars.

Set these two amounts equal to each other:
$$3x - 10 = x + 190$$
$$2x = 200$$
$$x = 100$$

12. **pencils = 10 cents each; notebooks = 15 cents each; erasers = 20 cents each:**

Let p = price of 1 pencil
Let n = price of 1 notebook
Let e = price of 1 eraser

Mehmet buys 3 pencils, 2 notebooks, and an eraser for 80 cents:
$$3p + 2n + e = 80$$
Gloria buys 5 pencils, 5 notebooks, and an eraser for $1.45:
$$5p + 5n + e = 145$$
Stan buys a pencil, a notebook, and an eraser for 45 cents:
$$p + n + e = 45$$

Combine equations (1) and (3) by subtraction to eliminate the variable e.

$$3p + 2n + e = 80$$
$$-\ p + \ n + e = 45$$
$$\overline{2p + \ n \ \ \ \ = 35}$$

Then, combine equations (2) and (3) by subtraction to eliminate the variable e.

$$5p + 5n + e = 145$$
$$-\ p + \ n + e = \ 45$$
$$\overline{4p + 4n \ \ \ \ = 100}$$

Then, combine the resulting 2-variable equations to isolate the variable n.

$$4p + 4n = 100$$
$$(2)(2p + \ n = 35) \quad \rightarrow \quad -\ 4p + 2n = \ 70$$
$$\overline{\quad\quad\quad 2n = \ 30}$$
$$n = \ 15$$

Finally, plug the known value for n into the 2-variable equation to get the value of p. Then, plug the known values of n and p into any of the original equations to get the value of e.

$$4p + 4n = 100 \qquad\qquad p + n + e = 45$$
$$4p + 4(15) = 100 \qquad\qquad 10 + 15 + e = 45$$
$$4p + 60 = 100 \qquad\qquad 25 + e = 45$$
$$4p = 40 \qquad\qquad\qquad e = 20$$
$$p = 10$$

13. **8:** Use an age chart to assign variables. Then write equations, using the information given in the problem:

	Now	in 3 years	in 5 years
Andrew	a	$a + 3$	$a + 5$
Larry	l	$l + 3$	$l + 5$
Jerome	j	$j + 3$	$j + 5$

(1) Andrew will be 1/2 as old as Larry in 3 years:

$$a + 3 = \frac{l + 3}{2}$$

(2) Jerome is 15 years older than Larry:

$$j = l + 15$$

(3) Andrew will be one-third as old as Jerome in 5 years:

$$a + 5 = \frac{j + 5}{3}$$

Eliminate the denominators in equations (1) and (3).

$$(1)\ a + 3 = \frac{l + 3}{2} \rightarrow 2a + 6 = l + 3 \qquad (3)\ a + 5 = \frac{j + 5}{3} \rightarrow 3a + 15 = j + 5$$

Solve equation (3) for j and set it equal to equation (2).

$$(3)\ j = 3a + 10 \qquad (2)\ j = l + 15$$

COMBINE: $3a + 10 = l + 15$

Then, combine this new equation with equation (1).

$$\begin{aligned} 3a + 10 &= l + 15 \\ -\ 2a + 6 &= l + 3 \\ \hline a + 4 &= 12 \\ a &= 8 \end{aligned}$$

14. **$125:** For this problem, it is helpful to make a chart to organize information. This will help you establish which information is unknown, so you can assign variables. Since the revenue from Standard tickets represents 1/3 of the total ticket revenue of $150,000, we can fill in $50,000 for the revenue from Standard tickets and $100,000 (the remainder) as revenue from VIP tickets.

	# sold	price	revenue
V.I.P.	n	v	100,000
Standard	$1.25n$	s	50,000

You know that there were a total of 1800 tickets sold. Using this information, solve for n and update the chart as follows:

$$n + 1.25n = 1800$$
$$2.25n = 1800$$
$$n = 800$$

	# sold	price	revenue
V.I.P.	800	v	100,000
Standard	1000	s	50,000

Lastly, solve for v: $800v = 100,000$
$$v = 125$$

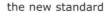

15. **Table - 2 years old; Aged - 62 years old; Vintage - 5 years old:**
Use an age chart to assign variables. Then write equations, using the information given in the problem:

	2 years ago	1 year ago	in 8 years
Aged	$a - 2$	$a - 1$	$a + 8$
Table	$t - 2$	$t - 1$	$t + 8$
Vintage	$v - 2$	$v - 1$	$v + 8$

8 years from now, 'Aged' will be 7 times older than 'Table.'
$\qquad$ (1) $a + 8 = 7(t + 8)$

1 year ago, 'Table' was one-fourth as old as 'Vintage.'
$\qquad$ (2) $t - 1 = \dfrac{v - 1}{4}$ Eliminate the denominator by multiplying by 4: $4t - 4 = v - 1$.

2 years ago, 'Aged' was 20 times older than 'Vintage.'
$\qquad$ (3) $a - 2 = 20(v - 2)$

Solve equation (1) for a and substitute this value into equation (3).
$\qquad a + 8 = 7t + 56 \qquad\qquad 7t + 48 - 2 = 20v - 40$
$\qquad a = 7t + 48 \qquad\qquad\quad 7t - 20v = -86$

Combine this equation with equation (2).
$$7t - 20v = -86$$
$$-20(4t - v = 3) \rightarrow \quad + \; -80t + 20v = -60$$
$$-73t \qquad\quad = -146$$
$$t = 2$$

Substitute this value for t into equation (1).
$\qquad a = 7t + 48$
$\qquad a = 7(2) + 48$
$\qquad a = 62$

Substitute this value for t into equation (2).
$\qquad 4t - v = 3$
$\qquad 4(2) - v = 3$
$\qquad v = 5$

*Manhattan*GMAT Prep
the new standard

Chapter 2
of
WORD TRANSLATIONS

RATES & WORK

In This Chapter . . .

- Basic Motion: The RTD Chart
- Matching Units in the RTD Chart
- Average Rate: Don't Just Add and Divide
- Simultaneous Motion Problems: Clicking Charts
- Assigning Variables in Simultaneous Motion Problems
- Basic Work Problems
- Working Together: Add the Rates
- Population Problems

RATES & WORK

The GMAT's favorite Word Translation type is the RATE problem. Rate problems come in a variety of forms on the GMAT, but all are marked by three primary components: RATE, TIME, & DISTANCE.

These three elements are related by the equation: Rate $\times$ Time = Distance. This equation can be abbreviated as $RT = D$. Basic rate problems involve simple manipulations of this equation.

Rate problems are often disguised in various forms. One of the most common types of rate problems in disguise is the WORK problem. Work problems are really rate problems because they involve a working rate, a time, and a distance. In Work problems, distance refers to the job performed (as opposed to a distance traveled).

Rate problems on the GMAT come in five main forms:
- (1) Basic Motion Problems
- (2) Average Rate Problems
- (3) Simultaneous Motion Problems
- (4) Work Problems
- (5) Population Problems

> For simple motion problems, use the equation $RT = D$. Simply plug in the values you know and solve for the unknown.

Basic Motion: The RTD Chart

All basic motion problems involve three elements: Rate, Time, and Distance.

Rate is expressed as a ratio of distance and time, with two units.
Some examples of rates include: 30 miles per hour, 10 meters/second, 15 kilometers/day.

Time is expressed using one unit.
Some examples of times include: 6 hours, 23 seconds, 5 months, etc.

Distance is expressed using one unit.
Some examples of distances include: 18 miles, 20 meters, 100 kilometers.

Fill in your RTD chart by reading the problem and finding two of the variables. Then, use the basic RTD formula to solve for the missing third variable. For example:

> **If a car is traveling at 30 miles per hour, how long does it take to travel 75 miles?**

When solving basic rate problems, create an RTD chart, as shown to the right. Fill in your RTD chart with the given information:

R	30 mph
T	
D	75 miles

*Manhattan*GMAT*Prep

Matching Units in the RTD Chart

It is imperative that all the units in your RTD chart match up with one another. The two units in the rate should match up with the unit of time and the unit of distance. For example:

> **It takes an elevator four seconds to go up one floor. How many floors will the elevator rise in two minutes?**

The rate is 1 floor/4 seconds, which simplifies to .25 floors/second. The time is 2 minutes. The distance is unknown.

R	.25 f/s
T	2 min
D	

Watch out! There is a problem with this RTD chart. The rate is expressed in floors per second, but the time is expressed in minutes. This will yield an incorrect answer.

To correct this table, we can change the time into seconds. Then all the units will match.

R	.25 f/s
T	120 s
D	

The time has been converted from 2 minutes to 120 seconds. Now the time unit matches the rate unit, and we can solve for the distance using the $RT = D$ equation: $.25(120) = d$ $d = 30$ floors

Another example:

> **A train travels 90 kilometers/hr. How many hours does it take the train to travel 450,000 meters?**

Notice that before entering the information into the RTD chart, we convert the distance from 450,000 meters to 450 km. This is necessary so that the distance unit matches up with the rate, which is expressed in kilometers per hour.

R	90 km/hr
T	
D	450 km

We can now solve for the time: $90t = 450$. Thus, $t = 5$ hours.

*Manhattan*GMAT°Prep
the new standard

Convert the units to match them up before you substitute the values into the RT = D equation.

Average Rate: Don't Just Add and Divide

Consider the following problem:

> **If Lucy walks to work at a rate of 4 miles per hour, and walks home by the same route at a rate of 6 miles per hour, what is Lucy's average walking rate for the round trip?**

It is very tempting to find an average rate as one would find any other average: add and divide. Thus, one would say that Lucy's average rate is 5 miles per hour ($4 + 6 = 10$ and $10 \div 2 = 5$). However, this is INCORRECT!

To find an average rate, you may not simply add the rates and divide, because Lucy walks at 4 miles/hour for more time than she walks at 6 miles/hour. In order to find the average rate, you must first find the TOTAL combined time for the trips and the TOTAL combined distance for the trips.

First, we need a value for the distance. Since all we need to know to determine the average rate is the *total time* and *total distance*, we can actually pick any number for the distance. The portion of the total distance represented by each part of the trip (GOING and RETURN) will dictate the time.

Pick a Smart Number for the distance. Since 12 is a multiple of the two rates in the problem, 4 and 6, 12 is an ideal choice.

Set up a Double Rate Chart:

	GOING	RETURN	TOTAL
R	4 mph	6 mph	
T			
D	12 miles	12 miles	24 miles

The times can be found using the *RTD* equation. For the GOING trip, $4t = 12$, so $t = 3$ hours. For the RETURN trip, $6t = 12$, so $t = 2$ hours. Thus, the total time is 5 hours, and we can complete the Double Rate Chart:

	GOING	RETURN	TOTAL
R	4 mph	6 mph	
T	3 hrs	2 hrs	5 hrs
D	12 miles	12 miles	24 miles

Now that we have the total TIME and the total DISTANCE, we can find the AVERAGE rate using the RTD formula:

$$RT = D$$
$$r(5) = 24$$
$$r = 4.8 \text{ miles per hour}$$

You can test this out with different numbers for the distance (try 24 or 36) to prove that you will get the same answer, regardless of the number you choose for the distance.

Manhattan **GMAT** Prep
the new standard

Simultaneous Motion Problems: Clicking Charts

The more difficult rate problems on the GMAT involve more than one rate. For example, in "meeting" problems, two vehicles travel at different rates in opposite directions, eventually meeting at some place in between. In "comparing" problems, you are asked to compare two rates. For example, you might see a problem in which one person is walking down the stairs while another is riding the elevator.

These more complex problems are all united by the fact that they require you to find a relationship between two different rates; hence, we call these SIMULTANEOUS MOTION problems. In order to solve these problems, you need to find relationships between the rate, time, and distance of the two people or vehicles in question. Note that finding a relationship does NOT necessarily mean finding an exact value. You should become adept at writing down relations by using variables.

Use these guidelines to assign variables in simultaneous motion problems.

Rate Relations:

> (1) If Train A is traveling at a certain speed, and Train B is traveling at double that speed, you can relate these as r for Train A, and $2r$ for Train B.

> (2) If Maurice walks at a constant rate, and Wendy follows him at a constant rate 1 mph slower, Maurice's rate is r miles/hour and Wendy's rate is $r - 1$ miles/hour.

Time Relations: *Be careful on Time Relations, as these can be confusing. Consider which vehicle is traveling for a longer time. This vehicle gets a variable plus a value.*

> (1) If Train A leaves 10 minutes after Train B, then Train A's time is t minutes and Train B's time is $t + 10$ minutes.
> *Remember that Train B is traveling for a longer time, so it gets a variable plus a value.*

> (2) If Maurice leaves an hour before Wendy, then Maurice is walking for time $t + 1$ hours, while Wendy is walking for t hours.
> *Remember that Maurice is walking for a longer time, so he gets a variable plus a value.*

Distance Relations:

> (1) If Train A and Train B are 100 miles apart and are traveling towards each other, how far will Train A have traveled when they meet? The distance Train A will have traveled is d miles, while the distance Train B will have traveled is $100 - d$ miles.

> (2) Jamal lives on a certain floor of a high-rise apartment building, and he can ride down the elevator or take the stairs. The distance for both the elevator and the stairs is d floors.

Use the following step-by-step method to solve Simultaneous Motion problems like this:

> **Stacy and Heather are 20 miles apart and walk towards each other along the same route. Stacy walks at a constant rate that is 1 mile per hour faster than Heather's constant rate of 5 miles/hour. If Heather starts her journey 24 minutes after Stacy, how far from her original destination has Heather walked when the two meet?**
> **(A) 7 miles (B) 8 miles (C) 9 miles (D) 10 miles (E) 12 miles**

	STACY	HEATHER	TOTAL
R	6 mph	5 mph	
T	$t + 24$ min	t min	
D	$20 - d$ miles	d miles	20 miles

1. Using a Double Rate Chart, fill in any values or relations between the two individuals. Also fill in any totals that you know.

	STACY	HEATHER	TOTAL
R	6 mph	5 mph	
T	$t + 4$ hours	t hours	
D	$20 - d$ miles	d miles	20 miles

2. Check to see that all your units match. If they do not, revise your chart. (Note that time was originally given in minutes, which did not match up with the rate units.)

Always use a double rate chart to solve simultaneous motion problems.

3. Use your ANSWER CHOICES to see which one makes the chart CLICK.

Answer choice (C) 9 miles. WRONG!   &   Answer choice (B) 8 miles. CORRECT!

	STACY	HEATHER	TOTAL
R	6	5	
T	$t + .4$	t	
D	11	9	20

	STACY	HEATHER	TOTAL
R	6	5	
T	$t + .4$	t	
D	12	8	20

Solving for Heather's time, $5t = 9$, $t = 1.8$ hours. However, this does not work when plugged into Stacy's time because $6(2.2) \neq 11$.

Solving for Heather's time, $5t = 8$, $t = 1.6$ hours. This CLICKS when plugged into Stacy's time because $6(2) = 12$.

Another strategy to solve these problems is to use the Double Rate Chart to set up two equations, which can be solved using substitution:

HEATHER   STACY
$5t = d$ $6(t + .4) = 20 - d$

COMBINE: $6t + 2.4 = 20 - 5t$
$$11t = 17.6$$
$$t = 1.6$$

Plug this value back into the $RT = D$ equation for Heather, and you will find that $d = 8$.

Assigning Variables in Simultaneous Motion Problems

The hardest part of solving simultaneous motion problems is assigning variables correctly. To assign variables for time, think about which person (or object) is traveling for a *longer* time. This person should be assigned a variable plus a number. To assign variables for distance, think about whether the two people are moving TOWARDS each other, AWAY from each other, or along the SAME PATH. The previous problem involved two girls traveling TOWARDS each other. Consider the problems below, in which two people move away from each other and then along the same path.

Draw a sketch of the motion. Then decide whether the two people or things are moving towards or away from each other.

Scott and Katie leave Penn Station at 2:00 P.M. Scott walks south at a rate of 3 miles per hour. Katie walks north at a rate of 4 miles per hour. At 5:00 P.M., how far apart from each other will Scott and Katie be?

In this problem, Scott and Katie are moving AWAY from each other. They travel for the same *time* but for different *distances*.

	SCOTT	KATIE	TOTAL
R	3 mph	4 mph	
T	t hours	t hours	
D	d_1 miles	d_2 miles	d miles

Katie leaves Scott's house at 2:00 P.M. She walks towards the park at a rate of 3 miles per hour. 30 minutes later, Scott realizes she has forgotten something and runs after her at a rate of 5 miles per hour. How far has Katie traveled before Scott catches up to her?

In this problem, Scott and Katie are moving along the SAME PATH. They travel for different *times* but for the same *distance*.

	SCOTT	KATIE	TOTAL
R	5 mph	3 mph	
T	t hours	$t + .5$ hours	
D	d miles	d miles	$2d$ miles

Use logical reasoning to assign the variables in simultaneous motion problems. Sometimes, the key to solving the problem lies in identifying the variable that is the *same* for both columns in the table.

Basic Work Problems

Work problems are just another type of rate problem. Just like all other rate problems, work problems involve three elements: rate, time, and distance.

WORK: In work problems, distance is replaced by work, which refers to the number of jobs completed or the number of items produced.

TIME: This is the time spent working.

RATE: In motion problems, the rate is a ratio of distance to time, or the amount of distance traveled in one time unit. In work problems, the rate is a ratio of work to time, or the amount of work completed in one time unit.

For example:

> **If a copier can make 3 copies every 2 seconds, how long will it take to make 40 copies?**

Here, the work is 40 copies, because this is the number of items produced. The time is unknown. The rate is 3 copies/2 seconds, or 1.5 copies per second.

> **If it takes Anne 5 hours to paint one fence, and she has been working for 7 hours, how many fences has she painted?**

Here the time is 7 hours, because that is the time which Anne spent working. The work done is unknown. Anne's working rate is 1 fence per 5 hours, or 1/5 fence per hour.

Basic work problems are solved like basic rate problems, using an RTW chart or the RTW equation. Simply replace the distance with the work. They can also be solved with a simple proportion. Here are both methods for Anne's work problem:

Treat work problems like motion problems. Use the $RT = W$ equation and pay close attention to your units.

RTW CHART

R	1/5 fnc/hr
T	7 hours
W	x

$$RT = W$$

$$\frac{1}{5}(7) = \frac{7}{5}$$

PROPORTION

$$\frac{5 \text{ hours}}{1 \text{ fence}} = \frac{7 \text{ hours}}{x \text{ fences}}$$

$$5x = 7$$

$$x = \frac{7}{5}$$

Anne has painted 1.4 fences.

Working Together: Add the Rates

The GMAT often presents problems in which there are multiple workers, working together to complete a job.

The trick to these "working together" problems is to determine the combined rate of all the workers working together. This combined working rate is equal to the sum of all the individual working rates. (Note: this is different from "average rate" problems in which you may not add rates.)

> **Larry can wash a car in 1 hour, Moe can wash a car in 2 hours, and Curly can wash a car in 4 hours. How long will it take them to wash a car together?**

First, find their individual rates, or the amount of work they can do in one hour: Larry's rate is 1 (or 1 car/1 hour), Moe's rate is 1 car/2 hours, and Curly's rate is 1 car/4 hours. To find their combined rate, sum their individual rates:

$$1 + \frac{1}{2} + \frac{1}{4} = \frac{7}{4} \text{ cars/hr.}$$

Then, create an RTW chart:

Using the formula $RT = W$, solve for the time:

$$RT = W$$

$$\frac{7}{4}t = 1$$

$$t = \frac{4}{7} \text{ hours, or approximately 34 minutes}$$

R	7/4 cars/hr
T	t
W	1 car

Population Problems

The final type of rate problem on the GMAT is the population problem. These can be solved with a population chart. Consider the following example:

> **The population of a certain bacteria triples every 10 minutes. If the population of a colony 20 minutes ago was 100, in approximately how long from now will the bacteria population reach 24,000?**

To solve this problem, use a population chart such as the one to the right. You can see from the chart that the bacteria population will reach 24,000 in about 30 minutes.

The key to population problems is to include NOW in the middle of your population chart. This allows you to work backward into the past *and* forward into the future.

Time Elapsed	Population
20 minutes ago	100
10 minutes ago	300
NOW	900
in 10 minutes	2,700
in 20 minutes	8,100
in 30 minutes	24,300

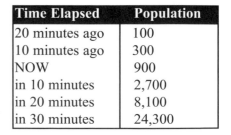

Problem Set

Solve the following problems, using the strategies you have learned in this section. Use a rate chart to organize the information in each problem.

1.   A cat travels at 60 inches/second. How long will it take this cat to travel 300 feet?

2.   Water is being poured into a tank so that the tank is being filled at the rate of approximately 4 cubic feet per hour. If the dimensions of the tank are 6 feet long, 4 feet wide, and 8 feet deep, how many hours will it take to fill up the tank?

3.   The population of grasshoppers doubles in a particular field every year. Approximately how many years will it take the population to grow from 2,000 grasshoppers to 1,000,000 or more?

4.   Two hoses are pouring water into an empty pool. Hose 1 alone would fill up the pool in 6 hours. Hose 2 alone would fill up the pool in 4 hours. How long would it take for both hoses to fill up two-thirds of the pool?

5.   One hour after Andrew started walking the 60 miles from X to Y, James started walking from X to Y as well. Andrew walks 3 miles per hour, and James walks 1 mile per hour faster than Andrew. How far from X will James be when he catches up to Andrew?
       (A) 8 miles (B) 9 miles (C) 10 miles (D) 11 miles (E) 12 miles

6.   Machine A produces widgets at a uniform rate of 160 every 40 minutes, and Machine B produces widgets at a uniform rate of 100 every 20 minutes. If the two machines run simultaneously, how long will it take them to produce 207 widgets in total?

7.   An empty bucket being filled with paint at a constant rate takes 6 minutes to be filled to 7/10 of its capacity. How much more time will it take to fill the bucket to full capacity?

8.   Three workers can Malk a Kow in 4, 5, or 6 minutes, respectively. How many Kows can be Malked by all three workers working together in 2 minutes?

9.   4 years from now, the population of a colony of bees will reach 1.6×10^8. If the population of the colony doubles every 2 years, what was the population 4 years ago?

10.   The Technotronic can produce 5 bad songs per hour. Wanting to produce bad songs more quickly, the record label also buys a Wonder Wheel, which works as fast as the Technotronic. Working together, how many bad songs can the two produce in 72 minutes?

11.   A car travels from Maxi to Priest at an average speed of 40 miles per hour, and returns immediately along the same route at an average speed of 50 miles per hour. What is the average speed in miles per hour for the round-trip?

12.   Jack is putting together gift boxes at a rate of 3 per hour in the first hour. Then Jill comes over and yells, "Work faster!" Jack, now nervous, works at the rate of only 2 gift boxes per hour for the next 2 hours. Then Alexandra comes to Jack and whispers, "The steadiest hand is capable of the divine." Jack, calmer, then puts together 5 gift boxes in the fourth hour. What is the average rate at which Jack puts together gift boxes over the entire period?

13.   Andrew drove from A to B at 60 miles per hour. Then he realized that he forgot something at A, and drove back at 80 miles per hour. He then zipped back to B at 90 mph. What was his approximate average speed in miles per hour for the entire night?

14.   A bullet train leaves Kyoto for Tokyo traveling 240 miles per hour at 12 noon. Ten minutes later, a train leaves Tokyo for Kyoto traveling 160 miles per hour. If Tokyo and Kyoto are 300 miles apart, at what time will the trains pass each other?
        (A)12:40 pm (B) 12:49 pm (C) 12:55 pm (D) 1:00 pm (E) 1:05 pm

15.   Nicky and Cristina are running a 1000 meter race. Since Cristina is faster than Nicky, she gives him a 12 second head start. If Cristina runs at a pace of 5 meters per second and Nicky runs at a pace of only 3 meters per second, how many seconds will Nicky have run before Cristina catches up to him?
        (A) 15 seconds   (B) 18 seconds   (C) 25 seconds   (D) 30 seconds (E) 45 seconds

1. **1 minute:** This is a simple application of the $RT = D$ formula, involving one unit conversion. First convert the rate, 60 inches/second, into 5 feet/second. Substitute this value for R. Substitute the distance, 300 feet, for D. Then solve:

$$(5 \text{ ft/s})(t) = 300 \text{ ft}$$

$$t = \frac{300 \text{ ft}}{5 \text{ ft/s}} = 60 \text{ seconds} = 1 \text{ minute}$$

R	5 ft/sec
T	t
D	300 ft

2. **48 hours:** The capacity of the tank is $6 \times 4 \times 8$, or 192 cubic feet. Use the $RT = D$ equation, substituting the rate, 4 ft^3/hour, for R, and the capacity, 192 cubic feet, for D.

$$(4 \text{ cubic feet/hr})(t) = 192 \text{ cubic feet}$$

$$t = \frac{192 \text{ cubic feet}}{4 \text{ cubic feet/hr}} = 48 \text{ hours}$$

R	4 ft^3/hr
T	t
D	192 ft^3

3. **9 years:** Organize the information given in a population chart. Notice that since the population is increasing exponentially, it doesn't take very long for the population to top 1,000,000.

Time Elapsed	Population
NOW	2,000
1 year	4,000
2 years	8,000
3 years	16,000
4 years	32,000
5 years	64,000
6 years	128,000
7 years	256,000
8 years	512,000
9 years	1,024,000

4. **1 3/5 hours:** If Hose 1 can fill the pool in 6 hours, its rate is 1/6, or the fraction of the job it can do in one hour. Likewise, if Hose 2 can fill the pool in 4 hours, its rate is 1/4. Therefore, the combined rate is 5/12 (1/4 + 1/6 = 5/12).

$$RT = W$$
$$5/12t = 2/3$$

R	5/12
T	t
W	2/3

5. **12 miles:** Organize this information in an RTD chart as follows:

	ANDREW	JAMES	TOTAL
R	3 mph	4 mph	
T	$t + 1$ hours	t hours	
D	d miles	d miles	$2d$ miles

You can use "clicking charts" by trying the answer choices one by one. Begin with (E) 12 miles, since 12 is a "smart number," a common multiple of the two rates given in the problem.

Alternately, you can set up algebraic equations to relate the information in the chart, using the $RT = D$ equation.

ANDREW: $3(t + 1) = d$ JAMES: $4t = d$

Substitute $4t$ for d in the first equation: $3(t + 1) = 4t$
                                                                            $3t + 3 = 4t$
                                                                            $t = 3$

                                           Therefore, $d = 4(3) = 12$ miles.

6. **23 minutes:** Machine A produces 160 widgets every 40 minutes; therefore, it produces 80 widgets every 20 minutes. Since Machine B produces 100 widgets every 20 minutes, together they will produce 180 widgets every 20 minutes, or 9 widgets per minute. Substitute this rate into the $RT = W$ equation, using the target work of 207 widgets for W:

(9 widgets/min.)t = 207 widgets
$t = 207 \div 9 = 23$ minutes

R	9 wid/min
T	t
W	207 wid

7. **$2\dfrac{4}{7}$ minutes:** Use the $RT = W$ equation to solve this problem, where $t = 6$ minutes and $w = .7$.

$r(6\text{ minutes}) = 7/10$
$r = 7/10 \div 6 = \dfrac{7}{60}$

R	r
T	6 min
W	7/10

Then, substitute this rate into the equation again, using 3/10 for w.

$\left(\dfrac{7}{60}\right)t = \dfrac{3}{10}$

$t = \dfrac{3}{10} \div \dfrac{7}{60} = \dfrac{18}{7} = 2\dfrac{4}{7}$ minutes

R	7/60
T	t
W	3/10

Manhattan GMAT® Prep
the new standard

8. **1 7/30 Kows:** Since this is a "working together" problem, add the individual rates:

$$\frac{1}{a} + \frac{1}{b} + \frac{1}{c} = \frac{1}{x}$$

$$\frac{1}{4} + \frac{1}{5} + \frac{1}{6} = \frac{1}{x}$$

Remember to find a common denominator:

$$\frac{15}{60} + \frac{12}{60} + \frac{10}{60} = \frac{37}{60}$$

> **Alternate Strategy: Add the Work**
> In 2 minutes, the first worker can Malk 1/2 a Kow. The second worker can Malk 2/5 a Kow. The third worker can Malk 1/3 a Kow. So in 2 minutes, all three workers together can Malk 37/30 Kows.

The 3 workers have a combined rate of 37/60 Kows per hour. Use the $RT = W$ equation to find the total work:

$$\left(\frac{37}{60}\right)(2 \text{ minutes}) = \frac{37}{30} = 1\frac{7}{30}$$

9. **1×10^7:** Organize the information given in a population chart.

Time Elapsed	Population
4 years ago	$.1 \times 10^8$
2 years ago	$.2 \times 10^8$
NOW	$.4 \times 10^8$
in 2 years	$.8 \times 10^8$
in 4 years	1.6×10^8

Then, convert:
$.1 \times 10^8 = 10,000,000 = 1 \times 10^7$

10. **12 songs:** Since this is a "working together" problem, add the individual rates: $5 + 5 = 10$

The two machines together can produce 10 bad songs in 1 hour. Then, use the $RT = W$ equation to find the total work done:

$(10)(1.2 \text{ hours}) = w$
$w = 12$ bad songs

R	10 sngs/hr
T	1.2 hr
W	w

11. **400/9 mph:** Use a double rate chart to solve this problem. Start by selecting a Smart Number for d: 200 miles. (This is a common multiple of the 2 rates in the problem.) Then, work backwards to find the time for each trip and the total time:

	Max to Pr	Pr to Max	TOTAL
R	40 mph	50 mph	
T	t_1 hours	t_2 hours	t
D	200 miles	200 miles	400 miles

$$t_1 = \frac{200}{40} = 5 \text{ hrs} \qquad t_2 = \frac{200}{50} = 4 \text{ hrs} \qquad t = 4 + 5 = 9 \text{ hours}$$

$$\text{The average speed} = \frac{\text{total distance}}{\text{total time}} = \frac{400}{9} \text{ mph.}$$

12. **3 boxes per hour:** The average rate is equal to the total work done divided by the time in which the work was done. Remember that you cannot simply average the rates. You must find the total work and total time. The total time is 4 hours. To find the total work, add up the boxes Jack put together in each hour: $3 + 2 + 2 + 5 = 12$. Therefore, the average rate is $\frac{12}{4}$, or 3 boxes per hour.

13. **≈ 74.5 mph:** Use a double rate chart to solve this problem. Start by selecting a Smart Number for d: 720 miles. (This is a common multiple of the 3 rates in the problem.) Then, work backwards to find the time for each trip and the total time:

$$t_A = \frac{720}{60} = 12 \text{ hrs}$$

$$t_B = \frac{720}{80} = 9 \text{ hrs}$$

$$t_C = \frac{720}{90} = 8 \text{ hrs}$$

	A to B	B to A	A to B	TOTAL
R	60 mph	80 mph	90 mph	
T	t_A hours	t_B hours	t_C hours	
D	720 miles	720 miles	720 miles	2,160 miles

$$t = 12 + 9 + 8 = 29 \text{ hours}$$

$$\text{The average speed} = \frac{\text{total distance}}{\text{total time}} = \frac{2160}{29} \approx 74.5 \text{ mph.}$$

*Manhattan*GMAT*Prep
the new standard

14. **12:49 P.M.:** This is a problem in which the trains are moving TOWARDS each other. Because the answer choices are given in times, instead of in hours, it is slightly more difficult to use the Clicking Charts strategy. Try solving this problem by writing algebraic equations:

	K to T	T to K	TOTAL
R	240 mph	160 mph	
T	$t + 1/6$ hours	t hours	
D	$300 - d$ miles	d miles	300 miles

K to T: $240(t + 1/6) = 300 - d$
$d = 300 - 240t - 40$
$d = 260 - 240t$

T to K: $160t = d$

COMBINE: $260 - 240t = 160t$
$260 = 400t$
$t = 39/60$ hours $= 39$ minutes

The first train leaves at 12 noon. The second train leaves at 12:10 P.M. 39 minutes after the second train has left, at 12:49 P.M., the trains pass each other.

15. **30 seconds:** This is a problem in which the people are moving in the SAME DIRECTION. You can use Clicking Charts or you can write algebraic equations. If you use Clicking Charts, it would be wise to try A, D, or E first, since they are all multiples of 5 and 3, the rates in this problem.

	Cristina	Nicky	TOTAL
R	5 m/s	3 m/s	
T	t seconds	$t + 12$ seconds	
D	d meters	d meters	

CRISTINA: $5t = d$

NICKY: $3(t + 12) = d$

COMBINE: $5t = 3(t + 12)$
$5t = 3t + 36$
$2t = 36$
$t = 18$

Therefore, Nicky will have run for 30 seconds before Cristina catches up to him.

Chapter 3
of
WORD TRANSLATIONS

RATIOS

In This Chapter . . .

RATIOS

A ratio expresses the relationship between two or more things.

Some ratios express a relationship between things with the same units:

> The two partners spend time working in the ratio of 1 to 3. For every 1 hour the first partner works, the second partner works 3 hours.

> Three sisters invest in a certain stock in the ratio of 2 to 3 to 8. For every $2 the first sister invests, the second sister invests $3, and the third sister invests $8.

Other ratios express a relationship between different things:

> The ratio of men to women in the room is 3 to 4. For every 3 men, there are 4 women.

> The crate is filled with apples, oranges, and peaches in the ratio of 1 to 4 to 5. For every 1 apple, there are 4 oranges and 5 peaches.

All ratios can be expressed in different ways:

> (1) Using the word "to," as in 3 to 4
>
> (2) Using a colon, as in 3:4
>
> (3) By writing a fraction, as in $\dfrac{3}{4}$

Finally, ratios can express a part-part relationship or a part-whole relationship:

> A part-part relationship: The ratio of men to women in the office is 3:4.
> A part-whole relationship: There are 3 men for every 7 employees.

It is very important to remember that ratios only express a *relationship* between two or more items; they do not provide enough information, on their own, to determine the exact quantity for each item. For example, knowing that the ratio of men to women in an office is 3 to 4 does NOT tell us exactly how many men and how many women are in the office.

In many ways, ratios behave just like fractions.

Label Each Part of the Ratio with Units

The order in which a ratio is given is vital. For example, saying, "the ratio of dogs to cats is 2:3" is very different from saying, "the ratio of dogs to cats is 3:2." The first ratio says that for every 2 dogs, there are 3 cats. The second ratio says that for every 3 dogs, there are 2 cats.

It is very easy to accidentally reverse the order of a ratio—especially on a timed test like the GMAT. Therefore, to avoid these reversals, always rewrite ratios as fractions with labels.

Thus, if the ratio of dogs to cats is 2:3, rewrite this as the labeled fraction $\dfrac{2 \text{ dogs}}{3 \text{ cats}}$.

If the ratio of dogs to cats is 3:2, rewrite this as the labeled fraction $\dfrac{3 \text{ dogs}}{2 \text{ cats}}$.

For ratios that involve more than two items, rewrite using a 3 part ratio or several labeled fractions. For example, if Arthur, Phillipe, and Maria paid for dinner in the ratio of 1 to 3 to 4, you can rewrite this using the 3 part ratio, 1:3:4, or using several labeled fractions as follows:

$$\frac{\$1 \text{ Arthur}}{\$3 \text{ Phillipe}} \qquad \frac{\$1 \text{ Arthur}}{\$4 \text{ Maria}} \qquad \frac{\$3 \text{ Phillipe}}{\$4 \text{ Maria}}$$

Proportions

Simple ratio problems can be solved with a proportion.

The ratio of girls to boys in the class is 4 to 7. If there are 35 boys in the class, how many girls are there?

Step 1: Set up a labeled PROPORTION:

$$\frac{4 \text{ girls}}{7 \text{ boys}} = \frac{x \text{ girls}}{35 \text{ boys}}$$

Step 2: Cross-multiply to solve:

$$140 = 7x$$
$$x = 20$$

Solve simple ratio problems with proportions.

The Unknown Multiplier

For more complicated ratio problems, it is helpful to think of a ratio as a fraction with an unknown multiplier for both the numerator and the denominator.

> **The ratio of men to women in a room is 3:4. If there are 56 people in the room, how many of the people are men?**

Thus, the ratio of men to women can be expressed as: $\dfrac{3x}{4x}$.

Here, x represents the "unknown multiplier". The key to ratio problems is to determine the value of this unknown multiplier.

$$\text{Men} + \text{Women} = \text{Total}$$
$$3x + 4x = 56$$
$$7x = 56$$
$$x = 8$$

For more complicated ratio problems, use the unknown multiplier.

Now we know that the value of x, the unknown multiplier, is 8. Therefore, we can determine the exact number of men and women in the room:

$$\dfrac{3x}{4x} = \dfrac{3(8)}{4(8)} = \dfrac{24}{32}$$

There are 24 men and 32 women in the room. This maintains the specified ratio of 3 men for every 4 women.

The ratio $\dfrac{3}{4}$ is just a way of expressing the actual fraction $\dfrac{24}{32}$ in lowest terms.

Here is another example where we need to first solve for the unknown multiplier:

> **A recipe calls for amounts of lemon juice, wine, and water in the ratio of 2:5:7. If all three combined yield 42 milliliters of liquid, how much wine was included?**

Write an EQUATION to solve for the unknown multiplier.

$$\text{Juice} + \text{Wine} + \text{Water} = \text{Total}$$
$$2x + 5x + 7x = 42$$
$$14x = 42$$
$$x = 3$$

Wine = $5x = 5(3) = 15$ milliliters.

Problem Set

Solve the following problems, using the strategies you have learned in this section. Use proportions and the unknown multiplier to organize ratios.

1.   48:2x is the equivalent of 144:600. What is x?

2. x:15 is the equivalent of y to x. Given that $y = 3x$, what is x?

3.   2x:y is the equivalent of 4x:8500. What is y?

4.   8:x^2 is the equivalent of 56:252. What is x?

5.   90:x is the equivalent of 3x^2: x^2. What is x?

6.   Brian's marbles have a red to yellow marble ratio of 2:1. If Brian has 22 red marbles, how many yellow marbles does Brian have?

7.   Initially, the men and women in a room were in the ratio of 5:7. 6 women leave the room. If there are 35 men in the room, how many women are left in the room?

8.   Initially, the men and women in a room were in the ratio of 4:5. Then, 2 men entered the room and 3 women left the room. Then, the number of women doubled. Now there are 14 men in the room. How many women are currently in the room?

9.   It is currently raining cats and dogs in the ratio of 5:6. If there are 18 fewer cats than dogs, how many dogs are raining?

10.   The amount of time that three people worked on a special project was in the ratio of 2 to 3 to 5. If the project took 110 hours, how many more hours did the hardest working person work than the person who worked the least?

11.   Alexandra needs to mix cleaning solution in the following ratio: 1 part bleach for every 4 parts water. When mixing the solution, Alexandra makes a mistake and mixes in half as much bleach as she ought to have. The total solution consists of 27 ml. How much bleach did Alexandra put into the solution?

12.   Initially, there are 32 people in a room, with a ratio of 5 men for every 3 women. 18 men leave, and the number of women in the room then diminishes, so that the number of women in the room is equal to twice the number of men in the room. In order to have a 2:1 ratio of men to women in the room, how many more men must be added?

13.   3 machines have a productivity ratio of 1 to 2 to 5. All 3 machines are working on a job for 3 hours. At the beginning of the 4th hour, the slowest machine breaks. It is fixed at the beginning of hour seven, and begins working again. The job is done in nine hours. What was the ratio of the work performed by the fastest machine as compared to the slowest?

14.   It takes the average dryer 80 minutes to dry one full load of Bob's laundry. Bob has one average dryer, and also decides to try one "Super Jumbo-Tron Dryer-Matic", which is faster than the average dryer by a ratio of 5:4. Bob has three loads of laundry, and both machines are so precise that he can set them to the minute. How many minutes does it take for him to dry his three loads? (Assume that no time passes between loads and that he can use both machines concurrently. Assume also that he never runs a machine with less than a full load.)

15.   4 sewing machines can sew shirts in the ratio 1:2:3:5. The fastest can sew a shirt in 2 hours. However, the fastest machine breaks. How long will it take the other three machines to sew a total of 3 shirts?

1. **100:**

$$\frac{48}{2x} = \frac{144}{600}$$ First, simplify the ratios on both sides of the proportion.

$$\frac{24}{x} = \frac{6}{25}$$ Then, cross-multiply: $6x = 600$.
Solve for x: $x = 600 \div 6 = 100$.

2. **45:**

$$\frac{x}{15} = \frac{y}{x}$$ First, substitute $3x$ for y.

$$\frac{x}{15} = \frac{3x}{x} = 3$$ Then, solve for x: $x = 3 \times 15 = 45$.

3. **4250:**

$$\frac{2x}{y} = \frac{4x}{8500}$$ First, simplify the ratio on the right-hand side of the equation.

$$\frac{2x}{y} = \frac{x}{2125}$$ Then, cross-multiply: $4250x = xy$.
Divide both sides of the equation by x: $y = 4250$.

4. **{−6, 6}:**

$$\frac{8}{x^2} = \frac{56}{252}$$ First, simplify the ratio on the right-hand side of the equation.

$$\frac{8}{x^2} = \frac{2}{9}$$ Then, cross-multiply: $2x^2 = 72$.
Divide both sides of the equation by 2: $x^2 = 36$.
Find the square root of both sides: $x = \{-6, 6\}$.

5. **30:**

$$\frac{90}{x} = \frac{3x^2}{x^2}$$ First, simplify the ratio on the right-hand side of the equation.

$$\frac{90}{x} = 3$$ Then, solve for x: $3x = 90$
$$x = 30$$

6. **11:** Write a proportion to solve this problem: $\dfrac{\text{red}}{\text{yellow}} = \dfrac{2}{1} = \dfrac{22}{x}$

Cross-multiply to solve: $2x = 22$
$$x = 11$$

7. **43:** First, establish the number of men and women that began in the room with a proportion:

$$\frac{5 \text{ men}}{7 \text{ women}} = \frac{35 \text{ men}}{x \text{ women}}$$ Cross-multiply and solve for x: $x = (35 \times 7) \div 5 = 49$.

If 6 women leave the room, there are $49 - 6 = 43$ women left.

8. **24:** Use the unknown multiplier to solve this problem. Initially, there are $4x$ men in the room and $5x$ women. Then, follow the series of entrances and exits one-by-one to establish the number of men and women who are currently in the room, in terms of x.

Men: $4x + 2 = 14$	**The unknown multiplier**	Women: $2(5x - 3) = ?$
$4x = 12$	**is 3. Plug 3 in for x.**	$2[5(3) - 3] = 2(12) = 24$
$x = 3$	$\longrightarrow$	

9. **108:** If the ratio of cats to dogs is 5:6, then there are $5x$ cats and $6x$ dogs. Express the fact that there are 18 fewer cats than dogs with an equation:

$$5x + 18 = 6x$$
$$x = 18$$

Therefore, there are $6(18) = 108$ dogs.

10. **33 hours:** Use an equation to represent the hours put in by the three people:

$$2x + 3x + 5x = 110$$
$$10x = 110$$
$$x = 11$$

Therefore, the hardest working person put in $5(11) = 55$ hours, and the person who worked the least put in $2(11) = 22$ hours. This represents a difference of $55 - 22 = 33$ hours.

11. **3 parts:** The correct ratio is 1:4, which means that there should be x parts bleach and $4x$ parts water. However, Alexandra put in half as much bleach as she should have, so she put in $\frac{x}{2}$ parts bleach. You can represent this with an equation: $\frac{x}{2} + 4x = 27$.

$x + 8x = 54$	The unknown multiplier is 6. Therefore,
$9x = 54$	Alexandra put $6 \div 2$, or 3 parts bleach into
$x = 6$	the solution.

12. **6:** First, use the unknown multiplier to find the total number of men and women in the room. The number of men is $5x$. The number of women is $3x$. If there are 32 people in the room, then:

$$5x + 3x = 32$$
$$8x = 32$$
$$x = 4$$

Initially, there are $5(4) = 20$ men and $3(4) = 12$ women in the room.

Then, 18 men leave, and there are 2 men and 12 women in the room. Finally, enough women leave so that there are twice as many women in the room as there are men. Since we know there are 2 men in the room, there must be only 4 women left. In order to have a men to women ratio of 2:1, there must be 8 men in the room, so 6 men must be added.

13. **15 to 2:** Machine A can produce x jobs in one hour; its rate of production is x. Machine B can produce $2x$ jobs in one hour; its rate of production is $2x$. Machine C can produce $5x$ jobs in one hour; its rate of production is $5x$. Machine C, the fastest machine, worked for 9 hours; use the $RT = W$ equation to calculate the work done: $5x(9) = 45x$. Machine A, the slowest machine, worked for 6 hours; use the $RT = W$ equation to calculate the work done: $x(6) = 6x$. The ratio of the work done by C to the work done by A is therefore 45 to 6, or 15 to 2.

14. **128 minutes:** The super dryer is faster than the average dryer by a ratio of 5:4. It takes the average dryer 80 minutes to dry a load; therefore, its rate is 1/80 of a load in a minute. Use a proportion to find the rate of the super dryer:

$$\frac{5}{4} = \frac{x}{1/80}$$

Cross-multiply: $5\left(\frac{1}{80}\right) = 4x$

$$x = \frac{1}{64}$$

It takes the super dryer 64 minutes to dry a load.

Assume that two of the three loads will be dried by the super dryer. This will take $2(64) = 128$ minutes. During those 128 minutes, the third load will be dried by the average dryer. However, since this is happening simultaneously, we do not need to add these 80 minutes.

15. **5 hours:** The first sewing machine can sew $1x$ shirts, the second can sew $2x$ shirts, the third $3x$ shirts, and the fastest machine $5x$ shirts. If the fastest machine can sew a shirt in 2 hours, its rate is 1/2 shirts/hr. We can use the rate of the fastest machine to solve for the unknown multiplier, x.

$$5x = \frac{1}{2}$$

$$x = \frac{1}{10}$$

However, recall that this machine is broken. To find the rates of the other machines, use the unknown multiplier x, which we now know is equal to one-tenth.

Machine 1: $1x = 1\left(\dfrac{1}{10}\right) = \dfrac{1}{10}$

Machine 2: $2x = 2\left(\dfrac{1}{10}\right) = \dfrac{2}{10}$

Machine 3: $3x = 3\left(\dfrac{1}{10}\right) = \dfrac{3}{10}$

Since this is a "working together" problem, add the individual rates: $\dfrac{1}{10} + \dfrac{2}{10} + \dfrac{3}{10} = \dfrac{6}{10}$

Together, Machines 1-3 can make 6/10 shirts in one hour. To find out how long it will take them to make 3 shirts, use the $RT = W$ equation:

$(6/10 \text{ shirts/hr})t = 3 \text{ shirts}$

$t = 3 \div \dfrac{6}{10} = 5 \text{ hours}$

R	6/10 s/hr
T	t
W	3 shirts

Chapter 4
of
WORD TRANSLATIONS

COMBINATORICS

In This Chapter . . .

COMBINATORICS

Combinatorics is the branch of mathematics that deals with questions like these:

(1) If there are 4 people and 4 chairs in a room, how many different seating arrangements are possible?
(2) If there are 7 people in a room, but only 4 chairs available, how many different seating arrangements are possible?
(3) If a team of 4 people is to be chosen from 7 people in a room, how many different teams are possible?

The three preceding questions are similar in that they ask you to find the total number of possibilities for a given situation. In essence, combinatorics is just advanced counting.

n factorial $= n! = n \times (n-1) \times (n-2) \times (n-3) \ldots \times 1$

Simple Factorials

The simplest combinatorics problems involve arranging a set of unique objects or people. For example:

If there are 4 people and 4 chairs in a room, how many different seating arrangements are possible?

In this problem, you have four choices for the person who will sit in the first chair. Once one person has been assigned to the first chair, you have three choices for the person who will sit in the second chair. Then you have two choices for the person in the third chair and one choice for the person in the last chair.

Therefore, there are $4 \times 3 \times 2 \times 1$ ways in which to seat 4 people in 4 chairs, or 24 ways. This multiplication pattern of decreasing integers can be written in shorthand as 4!, called "factorial."

For any number, n, $n!$ is calculated as follows: $n! = n(n-1)(n-2)(n-3).....(1)$.

Anagrams

Anagrams are different arrangements of the letters in a word (or words), usually to make a new word (or words). For example, you can rearrange the letters in the word LEVER to make the word REVEL. Anagrams are a very helpful model for understanding and solving combinatorics problems. However, for the purposes of the mathematical model, it does not matter whether or not an anagram makes sense as a word; we are merely concerned with the different arrangements of letters.

How many different anagrams can you make for the word GMAT?

GMAT	MGAT	AGMT	TGMA
GMTA	MGTA	AGTM	TGAM
GATM	MAGT	AMGT	TMGA
GAMT	MATG	AMTG	TMAG
GTMA	MTGA	ATGM	TAMG
GTAM	MTAG	ATMG	TAGM

Anagram problems can be solved with factorials.

A systematic list reveals 24 anagrams. The list-making process can be represented with a tree diagram, allowing us to see the mathematics behind the sum, 24.

Notice that there are 4 choices for the first letter in the anagram. Then, once that first letter is selected, there are only 3 choices for the second letter, since that first letter has already been used. There are only 2 choices for the third letter, and 1 choice for the last letter. The total number of branches in the tree then, is 4 × 3 × 2 × 1, or 24.

This explains why there are 24 anagrams for the word GMAT.

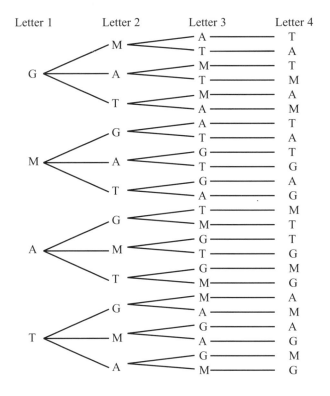

Seating Arrangements

Now let's consider the second combinatorics question we posed at the beginning of this section:

If there are 7 people in a room, but only 4 chairs available, how many different seating arrangements are possible?

In this problem, each of the 7 people in the room (A, B, C, D, E, F, and G) could be in seat #1, #2, #3, or #4 — or each could be one of the three people not seated in a chair. Let's assign these three people the designation N, to show that they are not seated. We can use N's to represent all three of the standing positions, since the order in which they are standing is not important to the problem.

We can set up a combinatorics grid to generate one of the possible permutations.

A	B	C	D	E	F	G
1	2	3	4	N	N	N

Divide by the factorial of the number of repeated letters.

Then the question is, in how many ways can we arrange these letters and numbers? This problem can be modeled with anagrams of the "word" 1234NNN.

Using the factorial logic from the previous section, it would appear that there are 7! anagrams for this "word." However, $1234N_1N_2N_3$ represents the same seat assignments as $1234N_3N_2N_1$. Although the two arrangements represent different mathematical permutations, they both mean that person A is seated in seat 1, person B is seated in seat 2, person C is seated in seat 3, person D is seated in seat 4, and people E, F, and G are not seated.

There are 3! ways in which you can arrange the three N's. Calculating 7! will give you 3! times as many anagrams as there really are. Since the order in which the non-seated people are standing is not important to the problem, we actually do not wish to count all the different arrangements of the three N's. In order to correct for this, we divide by 3!.

There are 7! ways to arrange 7 objects. However, since three of the objects are the same, you must divide by 3!.

$$\frac{7!}{3!} = \frac{7 \times 6 \times 5 \times 4 \times 3 \times 2 \times 1}{3 \times 2 \times 1} = 7 \times 6 \times 5 \times 4 = 840$$

There are 840 unique ways in which to seat 7 people in 4 chairs.

Always represent situations in which the order does not matter with repeated letters in your combinatorics grid. Then, divide by the factorial of the number of repeated letters to account for over-counting.

More Repeated Letters

Now consider the third problem from the beginning of this section:

If a team of 4 people is to be chosen from 7 people in a room, how many different teams are possible?

This problem is actually the simplest anagram of them all. Each person is either on the team or not on the team: yes or no.

A	B	C	D	E	F	G
Y	Y	Y	Y	N	N	N

If the order does not matter, use the letters Y and N to represent Yes and No situations.

This problem can be modeled with an anagram of the word "YYYYNNN." There are 7! ways to arrange 7 letters. However, since three of the letters are N's and four of the letters are Y's, you must divide by 3! and 4!.

$$\frac{7!}{4!3!} = \frac{7 \times 6 \times 5 \times 4 \times 3 \times 2 \times 1}{(4 \times 3 \times 2 \times 1)(3 \times 2 \times 1)} = \frac{7 \times 6 \times 5}{3 \times 2 \times 1} = 7 \times 5 = 35$$

There are 35 possible teams.

The Key To Combinations and Permutations

Problems such as the ones in this section are called combination and permutation problems. When the order does not matter, you are dealing with a combination. When the order does matter, you are dealing with a permutation.

It is not critical that you remember which problems are combinations and which are permutations. The key to solving either type of problem is to set up an anagram model to represent each person or object in the situation. Use numbers to represent people and objects when the order matters. Use Y and N (or other letters, if appropriate), to represent people and objects when the order doesn't matter.

Always remember to divide by $n!$ when there are n repetitions of a letter in the anagram model.

Combinations with Constraints

The most complex combination and permutation problems include constraints: one person refuses to sit next to another, for example.

> **Greg, Marcia, Peter, Jan, Bobby, and Cindy go to a movie and sit next to each other in 6 adjacent seats in the front row of the theater. If Marcia and Jan will not sit next to each other, in how many different arrangements can the six people sit?**

This is a simple permutation with one constraint: Marcia and Jan will not sit next to each other. To solve the problem, ignore the constraint for now. Just find the number of ways in which six people can sit in 6 chairs.

$6! = 6 \times 5 \times 4 \times 3 \times 2 \times 1 = 720$

Then, find the number of combinations in which Marcia and Jan ARE sitting next to each other. Marcia and Jan could occupy seats 1&2, 2&3, 3&4, 4&5, or 5&6.

	seat 1	seat 2	seat 3	seat 4	seat 5	seat 6
1&2	**M**	**J**	X	X	X	X
	J	**M**	X	X	X	X
2&3	X	**M**	**J**	X	X	X
	X	**J**	**M**	X	X	X
3&4	X	X	**M**	**J**	X	X
	X	X	**J**	**M**	X	X
4&5	X	X	X	**M**	**J**	X
	X	X	X	**J**	**M**	X
5&6	X	X	X	X	**M**	**J**
	X	X	X	X	**J**	**M**

Looking at the chart, we can see that for each pair of adjacent seats, there are 2! = 2 ways in which Marcia and Jan can be arranged. For example, in seat pair 3&4, Marcia could sit in seat #3 and Jan could sit in seat #4, OR Jan could sit in seat #3 and Marcia could sit in seat #4.

Regardless of where Marcia and Jan are sitting, for each seat pair there are 4! = 24 ways in which the other 4 people can be arranged.

Therefore, there are $2 \times 24 = 48$ permutations for each seat pair. Since there are 5 seat pairs, there are $5 \times 48 = 240$ permutations in which Marcia and Jan ARE sitting next to each other.

To find the number of permutations in which Marcia and Jan are NOT sitting next to each other, subtract:

$720 - 240 = 480$

*Manhattan*GMAT*Prep
the new standard

> Use this method to solve the more complex combination and permutation problems.

Combinations with Constraints: Alternate Method

Another way to solve this problem utilizes a more straightforward multiplication approach. However, generating the numbers for the multiplication involves some logical thinking.

Draw a diagram to show the row of 6 chairs. Then, begin with the people involved in the constraint. Let's begin with Jan.

Jan has **6** possible choices.
If Jan is the first to sit, she can sit in any of the 6 seats.

Marcia has **3** or **4** possible choices.
If Jan has chosen to sit in one of the two end seats (1 or 6), only one seat is off-limits to Marcia—the seat immediately adjacent to Jan. This leaves 4 remaining seat options for Marcia.

If Jan has chosen to sit in one of the four middle seats (2, 3, 4, or 5), exactly two seats are off-limits to Marcia—the two seats on either side of Jan. This leaves 3 remaining seats options for Marcia.

Thus, in 1/3 of the cases, Marcia will have 4 seat options and, in 2/3 of the cases, Marcia will have only 3 seat options.

After seating Jan and Marcia, seat the non-constrained people.

Greg has **4** possible choices.
Greg can sit in any of the 4 remaining chairs not occupied by Marcia or Jan.

Peter has **3** possible choices.
Peter can sit in any of the 3 remaining chairs.

Bobby has **2** possible choices.
Bobby can sit in either of the 2 remaining chairs.

Cindy has **1** possible choice.
Cindy must sit in the 1 remaining chair.

To compute the total number of permutations, find the product of the number of choices for each of the six people:

$$6 \times (1/3 \cdot 4 + 2/3 \cdot 3) \times 4 \times 3 \times 2 \times 1 = 480$$

There are 480 different ways in which Marcia and Jan will NOT sit next to each other.

> When solving combinatorics problems with this approach, be sure to begin with the people involved in the constraints.

Problem Set

Solve each problem by modeling the situation with an anagram. Remember to take repeated letters into account by dividing by $n!$, where n equals the number of times the letter is repeated.

1. In how many different ways can the letters in the word "LEVEL" be arranged?

2. Amy and Adam are making boxes of truffles to give out as wedding favors. They have an unlimited supply of 5 different types of truffles. If each box holds 2 truffles of different types, how many different boxes can they make?

3. A men's basketball league assigns every player a two-digit number for the back of his jersey. If the league uses only the digits 1-5, what is the maximum number of players that can join the league such that no player has a number with a repeated digit (e.g. 22), and no two players have the same number?

4. The Natural Woman, a women's health food store, offers its own blends of trail mix. If the store uses 4 different ingredients, how many bins will it need to hold every possible blend, assuming that each blend must have at least two ingredients? (Also assume that each bin can hold one and only one blend.)

5. A pod of 6 dolphins always swims single file, with 3 females at the front and 3 males in the rear. In how many different arrangements can the dolphins swim?

6. A delegation from Gotham City goes to Metropolis to discuss a limited Batman-Superman partnership. If the mayor of Metropolis chooses 3 members of the 7-person delegation to meet with Superman, how many different 3-person combinations can he choose?

7. A British spy is trying to escape from his prison cell. The lock requires him to enter one number, from 1-9, and then push a pair of colored buttons simultaneously. He can make one attempt every 3 seconds. If there are 6 colored buttons, what is the longest possible time it could take the spy to escape from the prison cell?

8. The New York Classical Group is designing the liner notes for an upcoming CD release. There are 10 soloists featured on the album, but the liner notes are only 5 pages long, and therefore only have room for 5 of the soloists. The soloists are fighting over which of them will appear in the liner notes, as well as who will be featured on which page. How many different liner note arrangements are possible?

9. The principal of a high school needs to schedule observations of 6 teachers. She plans to visit one teacher each day for a week, so she will only have time to see 5 of the teachers. How many different observation schedules can she create?

10. A second grade class is writing reports on birds. The students' teacher has given them a list of 6 birds they can choose to write about. If Lizzie wants to write a report that includes two or three of the birds, how many different reports can she write?

11. Every morning, Casey walks from her house to the bus stop, as shown to the right. She always travels exactly nine blocks from her house to the bus, but she varies the route she takes every day. (One sample route is shown.) How many days can Casey walk from her house to the bus stop without repeating the same route?

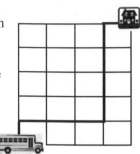

12. A mother bird has 6 babies. Every time she returns to the nest, she feeds half the babies. If it takes her 5 minutes to feed each baby, how long will it take her to feed all the possible combinations of three babies?

13. Mario's Pizza has two choices of crust: deep dish and thin-and-crispy. The restaurant also has a choice of 5 toppings: tomatoes, sausage, peppers, onions, and pepperoni. Finally, Mario's offers every pizza in extra-cheese as well as regular. If Linda's volley-ball team decides to order a pizza with four toppings, how many different choices do the teammates have at Mario's Pizza?

14. Three dwarves and three elves sit down in a row of six chairs. If no dwarf will sit next to another dwarf and no elf will sit next to another elf, in how many different ways can the elves and dwarves sit?

15. Gordon buys 5 dolls for his 5 nieces. The gifts include two identical Sun-and-Fun beach dolls, one Elegant Eddie dress-up doll, one G.I. Josie army doll, and one Tulip Troll doll. If the youngest niece doesn't want the G.I. Josie doll, in how many different ways can he give the gifts?

1. **30:** There are two repeated E's and two repeated L's in the word "LEVEL." To find the anagrams for this word, set up a fraction in which the numerator is the factorial of the number of letters and the denominator is the factorial of the number of each repeated letter.

$$\frac{5!}{2!2!} = \frac{5 \times 4 \times 3 \times 2 \times 1}{2 \times 1 \times 2 \times 1} = 30$$

2. **10:** In every combination, two types of truffles will be in the box, and three types of truffles will not. Therefore, this problem is a question about the number of anagrams that can be made from the "word" YYNNN:

A	B	C	D	E
Y	Y	N	N	N

$$\frac{5!}{2!3!} = \frac{5 \times 4 \times 3 \times 2 \times 1}{3 \times 2 \times 1 \times 2 \times 1} = 5 \times 2 = 10$$

3. **20:** In this problem, the order of the numbers matters. Each number can be either the tens digit, the units digit, or not a digit in the number. Therefore, this problem is a question about the number of anagrams that can be made from the "word" TUNNN:

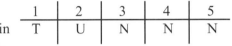

1	2	3	4	5
T	U	N	N	N

$$\frac{5!}{3!} = \frac{5 \times 4 \times 3 \times 2 \times 1}{3 \times 2 \times 1} = 5 \times 4 = 20$$

4. **11:** Trail mix blends can contain either 2, 3, or 4 ingredients. Consider each case separately. First, figure out the number of 2-ingredient blends as anagrams of the "word" YYNN:

A	B	C	D
Y	Y	N	N

$$\frac{4!}{2!2!} = \frac{4 \times 3 \times 2 \times 1}{2 \times 1 \times 2 \times 1} = 2 \times 3 = 6$$

Then, consider the number of 3-ingredient blends as anagrams of the "word" YYYN:

A	B	C	D
Y	Y	Y	N

$$\frac{4!}{3!} = \frac{4 \times 3 \times 2 \times 1}{3 \times 2 \times 1} = 4$$

Finally, consider the blend that includes all 4 ingredients. All in all, there are 6 + 4 + 1 = 11 blends. The store will need 11 bins to hold all the blends.

5. **36:** There are 3! ways in which the 3 females can swim. There are 3! ways in which the 3 males can swim. Therefore, there are 3! × 3! ways in which the entire pod can swim: 3! × 3! = 6 × 6 = 36.

6. **35:** Model this problem with anagrams for the "word" YYYNNNN, in which three people are in the delegation and 4 are not:

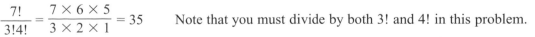

A	B	C	D	E	F	G
Y	Y	Y	N	N	N	N

$$\frac{7!}{3!4!} = \frac{7 \times 6 \times 5}{3 \times 2 \times 1} = 35$$ Note that you must divide by both 3! and 4! in this problem.

7. **6.75 minutes:** First, consider how many different pairs of colored buttons there are with the anagram YYNNNN:

A	B	C	D	E	F
Y	Y	N	N	N	N

$$\frac{6!}{4!2!} = \frac{6 \times 5 \times 4 \times 3 \times 2}{4 \times 3 \times 2 \times 2} = 3 \times 5 = 15$$

For each number the spy tries, he must then try all 15 button combinations. Therefore, there are 15 tries per number. With 9 numbers, there are $15 \times 9 = 135$ tries. If each try takes 3 seconds, it will take the spy a maximum of $135 \times 3 = 405$ seconds, or 6.75 minutes, to escape from the cell.

8. **30,240:** In this problem, the order in which the soloists appear is important. Therefore, the problem can be modeled with anagrams of the "word" 12345NNNNN, in which each number represents the page on which a soloist might appear:

A	B	C	D	E	F	G	H	I	J
1	2	3	4	5	N	N	N	N	N

$$\frac{10!}{5!} = 10 \times 9 \times 8 \times 7 \times 6 = 30,240$$

9. **720:** Model this problem with anagrams of the "word" 12345N, in which each teacher could be visited first, second, third, fourth, fifth, or not at all.

A	B	C	D	E	F
1	2	3	4	5	N

$6! = 6 \times 5 \times 4 \times 3 \times 2 \times 1 = 720$ Do not divide by anything, since no letters are repeated.

10. **35:** First, figure out the number of 2-bird reports as anagrams of the "word" YYNNNN:

$$\frac{6!}{4!2!} = \frac{6 \times 5}{2 \times 1} = 15$$

A	B	C	D	E	F
Y	Y	N	N	N	N

Then, consider the number of 3-bird reports as anagrams of the "word" YYYNNN:

$$\frac{6!}{3!3!} = \frac{6 \times 5 \times 4}{3 \times 2 \times 1} = 20$$

A	B	C	D	E	F
Y	Y	Y	N	N	N

All in all, there are $15 + 20 = 35$ possible bird combinations.

11. **126:** No matter which route Casey walks, she will travel 4 blocks to the left and 5 blocks down. This can be modeled with the "word" LLLLDDDDD. Find the number of anagrams for this "word":

$$\frac{9!}{5!4!} = \frac{9 \times 8 \times 7 \times 6}{4 \times 3 \times 2 \times 1} = 126$$

12. **5 hours:** The mother bird can feed 3 babies out of six. Model this situation with the "word" YYYNNN. Find the number of anagrams for this word:

$$\frac{6!}{3!3!} = \frac{6 \times 5 \times 4}{3 \times 2 \times 1} = 20$$

1	2	3	4	5	6
Y	Y	Y	N	N	N

If it takes 5 minutes to feed each baby, it will take 15 minutes to feed each combination of babies. Thus, it will take $20 \times 15 = 300$ minutes, or 5 hours, to feed all the possible combinations.

13. **20:** Consider the toppings first. Model the toppings with the "word" YYYYN, in which four of the toppings are on the pizza and one is not. The number of anagrams for this "word" is:

$$\frac{5!}{4!} = 5$$

A	B	C	D	E
Y	Y	Y	Y	N

If each of these pizzas can also be offered in 2 choices of crust, there are $5 \times 2 = 10$ pizzas. The same logic applies for extra-cheese and regular: $10 \times 2 = 20$.

14. **72:** The only way to ensure that no two dwarves and no two elves sit next to each other is to have the dwarves and elves alternate seats (DEDEDE or EDEDED). Begin by seating the first dwarf. As he is the first to be seated, he can sit anywhere. He has 6 choices. If the first dwarf sits in an odd-numbered chair, the second dwarf can sit in either of the two remaining odd-numbered chairs.

Person	Choices	Seat Assigned
Dwarf A	6 choices (1, 2, 3, 4, 5, 6)	#1
Dwarf B	2 choices (3, 5)	#3
Dwarf C	1 choice (5)	#5
Elf A	3 choices (2, 4, 6)	#2
Elf B	2 choices (4, 6)	#4
Elf C	1 choice (6)	#6

(Likewise, if the first dwarf sits in an even-numbered chair, the second dwarf can sit in either of the two remaining even-numbered chairs.) Either way, the second dwarf has two choices. The last dwarf has only 1 chair option, if he is not to be seated next to another dwarf.

Then, seat the elves. The first elf can sit in any of the three empty chairs, the second in any of the other two, and the last in the final remaining chair. Therefore, the first elf has three choices, the second elf has two choices, and the third elf has one choice.

Find the product of the number of choices for each person:

$$6 \times 2 \times 1 \times 3 \times 2 \times 1 = 72$$

15. **48:** First, solve the problem without considering the fact that the youngest girl doesn't want the G.I. Josie doll.

Gordon's nieces could get either one of the Sun-and-Fun dolls, which we'll call S. Or they could get the Elegant Eddie doll (E), the Tulip Troll doll (T), or the G.I. Josie doll (G). This problem can be modeled with anagrams for the "word" SSETG.

$$\frac{5!}{2!} = 5 \times 4 \times 3 = 60$$

A	B	C	D	E
S	S	E	T	G

Divide by 2! because of the two identical Sun-and-Fun dolls.

There are 60 ways in which Gordon can give the gifts to his nieces.

However, we know that the youngest girl (niece E) doesn't want the G.I. Josie doll. So, we calculate the number of arrangements in which the youngest girl DOES get the G.I. Josie doll. If niece E gets doll G, then we still have 2 S dolls, 1 E doll, and 1 T doll to give out to nieces A, B, C, and D. Model this situation with the anagrams of the "word" SSET:

$$\frac{4!}{2!} = 12$$

A	B	C	D
S	S	E	T

There are 12 ways in which the youngest niece WILL get the G.I. Josie doll.

Therefore, there are 60 − 12 = 48 ways in which Gordon can give the dolls to his nieces.

Chapter 5
of
WORD TRANSLATIONS

PROBABILITY

In This Chapter . . .

PROBABILITY

The probability of an event occurring is defined by a simple fraction relationship:

$$\frac{\text{\# of winning outcomes}}{\text{total \# of possible outcomes}}$$

The probability of rolling a "5" on one roll of a fair six-sided die:

$$\frac{\text{\# of winning outcomes}}{\text{total \# of possible outcomes}} = \frac{1}{6}$$ Here, there is only one "winner" (5) among six possible outcomes (1, 2, 3, 4, 5, 6).

The probability of flipping tails on a fair coin:

$$\frac{\text{\# of winning outcomes}}{\text{total \# of possible outcomes}} = \frac{1}{2}$$ Here, there is one "winner" (tails) between two possible outcomes (heads, tails).

To find probability, you need to know the total number of possibilities and the number of **winning scenarios**.

Probabilities can be expressed as fractions, percents, or decimals.

The probability of flipping tails $= \frac{1}{2} = 50\% = .5$

Since GMAT probability problems often involve some addition or multiplication, it is easiest to work with fractions. When a probability is expressed as a percent, it is often helpful to convert it into a fraction before proceeding with the problem. Note that when a probability is expressed as a fraction, it should be expressed in lowest terms.

"1" is the Greatest Probability

The greatest probability—the certainty that an event will occur—is 1. Thus, a probability of 1 means that the event must occur. For example:

The probability that you roll a fair die once, and it lands on a number less than seven, is certain, or 1. Using the probability fraction, we can see this:

$$\frac{\text{\# of winning outcomes}}{\text{total \# of possible outcomes}} = \frac{6}{6} = 1$$ There are six winners (1, 2, 3, 4, 5, 6) among six possibilities (1, 2, 3, 4, 5, 6).

As a percent, this certainty is expressed as 100%.

The converse is also true: The lowest probability—the impossibility that an event will occur—is 0. Thus, a probability of 0 means that an event will NOT occur. For example:

The probability that you roll a fair die once and it lands on the number 9 is impossible, or 0. Using the probability fraction, we can see this:

$$\frac{\text{\# of winning outcomes}}{\text{total \# of possible outcomes}} = \frac{0}{6} = 0$$ Here, there are no winners among six possibilities (1, 2, 3, 4, 5, 6).

As a percent, this impossibility is expressed as 0%.

More than One Event: "AND" vs. "OR"

Probability problems that deal with multiple events usually involve two operations: multiplication and addition. The key to understanding probability is to understand when you must multiply and when you must add.

Assuming that x and y are independent events: To determine the probability that event x AND event y will both occur, MULTIPLY the two probabilities together.

What is the probability that a fair coin flipped twice will land on heads both times?

This is an "and" problem, because it is asking for the probability that the coin will land on heads on both the first flip AND the second flip. The probability that the coin will land on heads on the first flip is 1/2. The probability that the coin will land on heads on the second flip is 1/2.

Therefore, the probability that the coin will land on heads on both flips is $\dfrac{1}{2} \times \dfrac{1}{2} = \dfrac{1}{4}$.

Alternatively, assuming that x and y are independent events and that they are mutually exclusive events (meaning that the two events, x and y, cannot both occur): To determine the probability that event x OR event y will occur, ADD the two probabilities together.

What is the probability that a fair die rolled once will land on either 4 or 5?

This is an "or" problem, because it is asking for the probability that the die will land on either 4 **or** 5. The probability that the die will land on 4 is 1/6. The probability that the die will land on 5 is 1/6.

Therefore, the probability that the die will land on either 4 or 5 is $\dfrac{1}{6} + \dfrac{1}{6} = \dfrac{1}{3}$.

Note: If x and y are independent events but are <u>not</u> mutually exclusive (meaning that both events can occur), the "or" formula is slightly different: Add the probabilities that each event occurs, and then subtract the probability that both events occur together.

A fair die is rolled once and a fair coin is flipped once. What is the probability that either the die will land on 3 or that the coin will land on heads?

These events are not mutually exclusive, since both can occur. The probability that the die will land on 3 is 1/6. The probability that the coin will land on heads is 1/2.

The probability of both these events occurring is $\dfrac{1}{6} \times \dfrac{1}{2} = \dfrac{1}{12}$.

Therefore, the probability of either event occurring is $\left(\dfrac{1}{6} + \dfrac{1}{2}\right) - \dfrac{1}{12} = \dfrac{7}{12}$.

AND means multiply the probabilities.
OR means add the probabilities.

*Manhattan*GMAT Prep
the new standard

The $1 - x$ Probability Trick

Often GMAT probability problems will be too time-consuming to solve by actually determining the probability that a certain event will happen. A simple trick can help you save time: Instead of finding the probability that an event will happen, find the probability that an event WILL NOT happen.

How does this help you? Consider this simple equation:

Probability that event will happen + Probability that event will not happen = 1

Once you know the probability that an event will not happen (we'll call this *x*), you can subtract this probability from 1 to determine the probability that the event will happen: $1 - x$.

For example:

What is the probability that, on three rolls of a single fair die, at least one of the rolls will be a six?

We could list all the possible outcomes of three rolls of a die (1-1-1, 1-1-2, 1-1-3, etc.), and then determine how many of them have at least one six, but this would be very time-consuming. Instead, it is easier to think of this problem in reverse before solving:

What is the probability that not one of the rolls will yield a 6?

On each roll, there is a $\frac{5}{6}$ probability that the die will not yield a 6.

Thus, the probability that on all 3 rolls the die will not yield a 6 is $\frac{5}{6} \times \frac{5}{6} \times \frac{5}{6} = \frac{125}{216}$.

Now we return to answer the question by subtracting our result from 1. The probability that at least one of the rolls will be a 6 includes every outcome, except when three consecutive non-sixes are rolled.

$1 - \dfrac{125}{216} = \dfrac{91}{216}$ is the probability that at least one six will be rolled.

Sometimes it is easier to calculate the probability that an event will NOT happen than the probability that the event WILL happen.

The Domino Effect

Sometimes the outcome of the first event will affect the probability of a subsequent event. For example:

In a box with 10 blocks, 3 of which are red, what is the probability of picking out a red block on your first two tries?

Since this is an "AND" problem, we must find the probability of both events and multiply them together. Consider how easy it is to make the following mistake:

The probability of picking a red block on your first pick is $\frac{3}{10}$.

The probability of picking a red block on your second pick is $\frac{3}{10}$.

Therefore, the probability of picking a red block on both picks is $\frac{3}{10} \times \frac{3}{10} = \frac{9}{100}$.

The solution above is WRONG, because it does not take into account that the first event affects the second event. If a red block is chosen on the first pick, then the number of blocks now in the box has decreased from **10 to 9**. Additionally, the number of red blocks now in the box has decreased from **3 to 2**. Therefore, the probability of choosing a red block on the second pick is different from the probability of choosing a red block on the first pick.

The correct solution to this problem is as follows:

The probability of picking a red block on your first pick is $\frac{3}{10}$.

The probability of picking a red block on your second pick is $\frac{2}{9}$.

Therefore, the probability of picking a red block on both picks is $\frac{3}{10} \times \frac{2}{9} = \frac{6}{90} = \frac{1}{15}$.

Do not forget to analyze events by considering whether one event affects subsequent events. The first roll of a die or flip of a coin has no affect on any subsequent rolls or flips. However, the first pick of an object out of a box does affect subsequent picks.

> Be careful of situations in which the outcome of the first event affects the probability of the second event.

Tough Probability: List the Winning Scenarios

Many high-level probability problems involve both "AND" and "OR" situations.

Renee has a bag of candy. The bag has 1 candy bar, 2 lollipops, 3 jelly beans, and 4 truffles. Jack takes one piece of candy out of the bag at random. If he picks a jellybean, he chooses one additional piece of candy and then stops. If he picks any non-jellybean candy, he stops picking immediately. After Jack picks his candy, Renee will pick a piece of candy. What is the probability that Renee picks a jellybean?

This problem involves multiple chains of complex events. You can simplify the possible events in problems like this by listing only the "winning" scenarios, or the scenarios that result in the specified outcome.

JACK (1)	JACK (2)	RENEE
jellybean	non-jellybean	jellybean
jellybean	jellybean	jellybean
non-jellybean	-	jellybean

List the winning scenarios to solve tough probability problems.

The next step is to calculate the probability of each "winning" event. As each "winning" scenario is an AND situation, multiply the probability of each independent event to find the probability of the chain. (Don't forget the Domino Effect, as Jack's picks affect the number of jellybeans and of candies in total left for Renee.)

Jack (Pick 1)	Jack (Pick 2)	Renee	Probability
(1) Jellybean $P = \dfrac{3}{10}$	Non-jellybean $P = \dfrac{7}{9}$	Jellybean $P = \dfrac{2}{8}$	$P = \left(\dfrac{3}{10}\right)\left(\dfrac{7}{9}\right)\left(\dfrac{2}{8}\right) = \dfrac{42}{720}$
(2) Jellybean $P = \dfrac{3}{10}$	Jellybean $P = \dfrac{2}{9}$	Jellybean $P = \dfrac{1}{8}$	$P = \left(\dfrac{3}{10}\right)\left(\dfrac{2}{9}\right)\left(\dfrac{1}{8}\right) = \dfrac{6}{720}$
(3) Non-jellybean $P = \dfrac{7}{10}$		Jellybean $P = \dfrac{3}{9}$	$P = \left(\dfrac{7}{10}\right)\left(\dfrac{3}{9}\right) = \dfrac{21}{90} = \dfrac{168}{720}$

The probability of either event chain (1) OR (2) OR (3) happening is the sum of the individual probabilities:

$$\frac{42}{720} + \frac{6}{720} + \frac{168}{720} = \frac{216}{720} = \frac{3}{10}$$

Manhattan **GMAT** Prep
the new standard

Tough Probability: Use Counting Methods

Another strategy for tough probability problems is to use combinatorics counting methods to count both the total number of possibilities and the number of winning scenarios, and then to set up a fraction to represent the probability.

Kate and her twin sister Amy want to be on the same relay-race team. There are 6 girls in the group, and only 4 of them will be placed on the team. What is the probability that Kate and Amy will both be on the team?

The winning scenario method, discussed in the previous section, involves finding the probability of each winning scenario. The 12 winning scenarios are shown to the right. The next step in this method would be to calculate the probability of each winning scenario and then to add all the probabilities.

Pick (1)	Pick (2)	Pick(3)	Pick (4)
Kate	Amy	X	X
Amy	Kate	X	X
X	Kate	Amy	X
X	Amy	Kate	X
X	X	Kate	Amy
X	X	Amy	Kate
Kate	X	X	Amy
Amy	X	X	Kate
Kate	X	Amy	X
Amy	X	Kate	X
X	Kate	X	Amy
X	Amy	X	Kate

As you can see, this method would be tedious in this problem. Instead, we can solve this problem using the counting methods described in the section on combinatorics.

Create a combinatorics grid to find the number of different 4-person teams:

A	B	C	D	E	F
Y	Y	Y	Y	N	N

There are $\frac{6!}{4!2!} = 15$ different teams.

Each of the winning scenarios will include Kate and Amy, plus 2 of the remaining 4 girls. Therefore, we can find the number of winning scenarios by using a combinatorics grid to tell us how many ways it is possible to choose 2 of the remaining 4 girls:

A	B	C	D
Y	Y	N	N

There are $\frac{4!}{2!2!} = 6$ winning scenarios.

Alternately, you can list the winning teams:

Kate, Amy, A, B   Kate, Amy, B, C
Kate, Amy, A, C   Kate, Amy, B, D
Kate, Amy, A, D   Kate, Amy, C, D

Therefore, the probability is 6/15, or 2/5.

Problem Set

Solve the following problems. Express probabilities as fractions or percentages unless otherwise instructed.

1.   What is the probability that the sum of two dice will yield a 4 or 6?

2.   What is the probability that the sum of two dice will yield anything but an 8?

3.   What is the probability that the sum of two dice will yield a 10 or lower?

4.   What is the probability that the sum of two dice will yield a 7, and then when both are thrown again, their sum will again yield a 7?

5.   What is the probability that the sum of two dice will yield a 5, and then when both are thrown again, their sum will yield a 9?

6.   There is a 30% chance of rain and a 70% chance of shine. If it rains, there is a 50% chance that Bob will cancel his picnic. What is the chance that Bob will have his picnic?

7.   At a certain pizzeria, 1/6 of the pizzas sold in a week were cheese, and 1/5 of the OTHER pizzas sold were pepperoni. If Zach bought a pizza from the pizzeria that week, what is the probability that he ordered a pepperoni?

8.   When a diver dives, there is a 20% chance of a perfect score. However, if a perfect score is given out, the judges won't give out another. Janet is the third diver to dive. What is the chance of Janet receiving a perfect score?

9.   In a bag of marbles, there are 3 red, 2 white, and 5 blue. If Bob takes 2 marbles out of the bag, what is the probability that he will have one white and one blue marble?

10. A florist has 2 azaleas, 3 buttercups, and 4 petunias. She puts two flowers together at random in a bouquet. However, the customer calls and says that she doesn't want two of the same flower. What is the probability that the florist doesn't have to change the bouquet?

11. One week a certain vehicle rental outlet had a total of 40 cars, 12 trucks, 28 vans, and 20 SUV's available. Andre and Barbara went to the vehicle rental outlet and chose 2 vehicles at random, with the condition that Andre and Barbara would not select two of the same type of vehicle (in other words, if one of them has an SUV, the other won't take an SUV, so the second person doesn't even consider the SUV's). What is the probability that, of the two vehicles, one of them is a car or a van?

12. Five A-list actresses are vying for the three leading roles in the new film, "Catfight in Denmark." The actresses are Julia Robards, Meryl Strep, Sally Fieldstone, Lauren Bake-all, and Hallie Strawberry. Assuming that no actress has any advantage in getting any role, what is the probability that Julia and Hallie will star in the film together?

Manhattan **GMAT** Prep

13.   A polling company reports that there is a 40% chance that a certain candidate will win the next election. If the candidate wins, there is a 60% chance that she will sign Bill X and no other bills. If she decides not to sign Bill X, she will sign either Bill Y or Bill Z, chosen randomly. What is the chance that the candidate will sign Bill Z?

14.   A magician has five animals in his magic hat: 3 doves and 2 rabbits. If he pulls two animals out of the hat at random, what is the chance that he will have a matched pair?

15.   If Lauren, Mary, Nancy, Oprah, and Penny sit randomly in a row, what is the probability that Oprah and Penny are NOT next to each other?

1. **2/9:** : There are 36 ways in which 2 dice can be thrown ($6 \times 6 = 36$). The combinations that yield sums of 4 and 6 are $1 + 3$, $2 + 2$, $3 + 1$, $1 + 5$, $2 + 4$, $3 + 3$, $4 + 2$, and $5 + 1$: 8 different combinations. Therefore, the probability is 8/36, or 2/9.

2. **31/36:** Solve this problem by calculating the probability that the sum WILL yield a sum of 8, and then subtract the result from 1. There are 5 combinations of 2 dice that yield a sum of 8: $2 + 6$, $3 + 5$, $4 + 4$, $5 + 3$, and $6 + 2$. (Note that $7 + 1$ is not a valid combination, as there is no 7 on a standard die.) Therefore, the probability that the sum will be 8 is 5/36, and the probability that the sum will NOT be 8 is $1 - 5/36$, or 31/36.

3. **11/12:** Solve this problem by calculating the probability that the sum will be higher than 10, and subtract the result from 1. There are 3 combinations of 2 dice that yield a sum higher than 10: $5 + 6$, $6 + 5$, and $6 + 6$. Therefore, the probability that the sum will be higher than 10 is 3/36, or 1/12. The probability that the sum will be 10 or lower is $1 - 1/12 = 11/12$.

4. **1/36:** There are 36 ways in which 2 dice can be thrown ($6 \times 6 = 36$). The combinations that yield a sum of 7 are $1 + 6$, $2 + 5$, $3 + 4$, $4 + 3$, $5 + 2$, and $6 + 1$: 6 different combinations. Therefore, the probability of rolling a 7 is 6/36, or 1/6. To find the probability that this will happen twice in a row, multiply $1/6 \times 1/6$: 1/36.

5. **1/81:** First, find the individual probability of each event. The probability of rolling a 5 is 4/36, or 1/9, since there are 4 ways to roll a sum of 5 ($1 + 4$, $2 + 3$, $3 + 2$, and $4 + 1$). The probability of rolling a 9 is also 4/36, or 1/9, since there are 4 ways to roll a sum of 9 ($3 + 6$, $4 + 5$, $5 + 4$, and $6 + 3$). To find the probability that both events will happen in succession, multiply $1/9 \times 1/9$: 1/81.

6. **85%:** There are two possible chains of events in which Bob will have the picnic:

One: The sun shines: $P = 7/10 = 14/20$ **OR**
Two: It rains AND Bob chooses to have the picnic anyway: $P = (3/10)(1/2) = 3/20$

Add the probabilities together to find the total probability that Bob will have the picnic:
$14/20 + 3/20 = 17/20 = 85\%$

7. **1/6:** If 1/6 of the pizzas were cheese, 5/6 of the pizzas were not. 1/5 of these 5/6 were pepperoni. Multiply to find the total portion: $1/5 \times 5/6 = 1/6$. If 1/6 of the pizzas were pepperoni, there is a 1/6 chance that Zach bought a pepperoni pizza.

8. **12.8%:** In order for Janet to receive a perfect score, neither of the previous two divers can receive one. Therefore, we are finding the probability of a chain of three events: that diver one will not get a perfect score AND diver two will not get a perfect score AND Janet will get a perfect score. Multiply the probabilities: $8/10 \times 8/10 \times 2/10 = 128/1000 = 12.8\%$

There is a 12.8% chance that Janet will receive a perfect score.

9. **2/9:** You can solve this problem by listing the winning scenarios or by using combinatorics counting methods. Both solutions are presented below:

(1) LIST THE WINNING SCENARIOS.

First Pick	Second Pick	Probability
(1) Blue (1/2)	White (2/9)	$1/2 \times 2/9 = 1/9$
(2) White (1/5)	Blue (5/9)	$1/5 \times 5/9 = 1/9$

To find the probability, add the probabilities of the winning scenarios: $1/9 + 1/9 = 2/9$.

(2) USE COUNTING METHODS.

A	B	C	D	E	F	G	H	I	J
Y	Y	N	N	N	N	N	N	N	N

There are $\dfrac{10!}{2!8!} = 45$ different combinations of marbles.

Since there are 2 white marbles and 5 blue marbles, there are $2 \times 5 = 10$ different white-blue combinations. Therefore, the probability of selecting a blue and white combination is 10/45, or 2/9.

10. **13/18:** Solve this problem by finding the probability that the two flowers in the bouquet WILL be the same, and then subtract the result from 1. The table to the right indicates that there are 10 different bouquets in which both flowers are the same. Then, find the number of different 2-flower bouquets that can be made in total, using an anagram model. In how many different ways can you arrange the letters in the "word" YYNNNNNNN?

$$\frac{9!}{7!2!} = \frac{9 \times 8}{2 \times 1} = 36$$

Flower #1	Flower #2
A_1	A_2
B_1	B_2
B_1	B_3
B_2	B_3
P_1	P_2
P_1	P_3
P_1	P_4
P_2	P_3
P_2	P_4
P_3	P_4

The probability of randomly putting together a bouquet that contains two of the same type of flower is 10/36, or 5/18. Therefore, the probability of randomly putting together a bouquet that contains two different flowers and that therefore will NOT need to be changed is $1 - 5/18$, or 13/18.

11.   **1037/1100:** Solve this problem by finding the probability that the combination of vehicles will NOT include either a car or a van. The only way this will happen is if Andre selects a truck and Barbara selects an SUV, OR if Andre selects an SUV and Barbara selects a truck.

	Andre	Barbara	Probability
(1)	Truck (12/100)	SUV (20/88)*	$12/100 \times 20/88 = 3/110$
(2)	SUV (20/100)	Truck (12/80)*	$20/100 \times 12/80 = 3/100$

The probability that either one OR the other of these events will happen is $3/110 + 3/100 = 63/1100$. The probability that neither of the "losing" cases will occur, and that the combination WILL have either a car or a van in it is:

$1 - 63/1100$, or 1037/1100

*Recall that Barbara will not pick the vehicle that Andre picks. Do not include these cases in the total.

12. **3/10:** The probability of Julia being cast first is 1/5. If Julia is cast, the probability of Hallie being cast second is 1/4. The probability of any of the remaining 3 actresses being cast is 3/3, or 1. Therefore, the probability of this chain of events is:

Actress (1)	Actress (2)	Actress (3)
Julia	Hallie	X
Julia	X	Hallie
Hallie	Julia	X
Hallie	X	Julia
X	Julia	Hallie
X	Hallie	Julia

$$1/5 \times 1/4 \times 1 = 1/20$$

There are six event chains that yield this outcome, shown in the chart to the right. Therefore, the total probability that Julia and Hallie will be among the 3 leading actresses is:

$$1/20 \times 6 = 6/20 = 3/10$$

Alternately, you can solve this problem with counting methods.

A	B	C	D	E
Y	Y	Y	N	N

The number of different combinations in which the actresses can be cast in the roles, assuming we are not concerned with which actress is given which role, is $\dfrac{5!}{3!2!} = 10$.

There are 3 possible combinations that feature both Julia and Hallie:

    (1) Julia, Hallie, Sally
    (2) Julia, Hallie, Meryl
    (3) Julia, Hallie, Lauren

Therefore, the probability that Julia and Hallie will star together is $\dfrac{3}{10}$.

13. **8%:** In order for the candidate to sign Bill Z, the following chain of events would need to take place:

    (1) She would have to win the election.
    (2) She would have to decide not to sign Bill X.
    (3) She would have to decide to sign Bill Z.

Assign each independent event a probability:

    (1) There is a 40% chance that she will win the election   AND
    (2) There is a 40% chance that she will not sign Bill X   AND
    (3) There is a 50% chance that she will sign Bill Z.

Multiply the probabilities of each event to find the probability that the entire event chain will occur:

$$\frac{4}{10} \times \frac{4}{10} \times \frac{5}{10} = \frac{80}{1000} = 8\%$$

There is an 8% chance that the candidate will sign Bill Z.

14. **40%:** Use an anagram model to find out the total number of different pairs the magician can pull out of his hat. Since two animals will be in the pair and the other three will not, use the "word" YYNNN.

A	B	C	D	E
Y	Y	N	N	N

$$\frac{5!}{2!3!} = \frac{5 \times 4}{2 \times 1} = 10$$ There are 10 possible pairs.

Then, list the pairs in which the animals will match. Let's represent the rabbits with the letters A and B, and the doves with the letters X, Y, and Z.

Matched Pairs:
RaRb
DxDy   There are four pairs in which the animals will be
DxDz   a matched set.
DyDz

Therefore, the probability that the magician will randomly draw a matched set is $\frac{4}{10} = 40\%$.

15. **3/5:** Use counting methods to find the total number of ways in which the five girls can sit.

A	B	C	D	E
1	2	3	4	5

There are 5! = 120 ways in which the five girls can sit.

It is simpler to find the arrangements in which Oprah and Penny ARE next to each other than the ones in which they are NOT next to each other.

OPXXX	XOPXX	XXOPX	XXXOP
POXXX	XPOXX	XXPOX	XXXPO

There are 8 arrangements in which Oprah and Penny are next to each other. For each of these arrangements, there are 3! = 6 ways in which the three other girls can be arranged.

$$6 \times 8 = 48$$

Therefore, the probability that Oprah and Penny WILL sit next to each other is $\frac{48}{120}$, or $\frac{2}{5}$.

The probability that Oprah and Penny will NOT sit next to each other is $1 - \frac{2}{5} = \frac{3}{5}$.

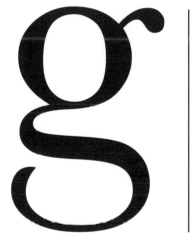

Chapter 6
of
WORD TRANSLATIONS

STATISTICS

In This Chapter . . .

AVERAGES

The average (or the arithmetic mean) of a set is determined by the formula:

$$\text{Average} = \frac{\text{Sum}}{\text{\# of terms}}, \text{ which is abbreviated as } A = \frac{S}{n}.$$

The sum, S, refers to the sum of all the terms in the set.
The number, n, refers to the number of terms that are in the set.
The average, A, refers to the average value of the terms in the set.

Every single GMAT problem that deals with average can be solved by utilizing the average formula or some variation upon it. The key to most average problems is to understand that, to find the average, you do not need to know each individual term in the set; you only need to know the sum of the terms.

Using the Average Formula

The first thing to do for any GMAT average problem is to write down the average formula. Then, fill in any of the 3 variables (S, n, and A) that are given in the problem.

The sum of 6 numbers is 90. What is the average term?

$$A = \frac{S}{n}$$

The sum, S, is given as 90. The number of terms, n, is given as 6.
By plugging in, we can solve for the average: $\frac{90}{6} = 15$

Notice that one does NOT need to know each term in the set to find the average!

Sometimes, using the average formula will be more involved. For example:

If the average of the set {2, 5, 5, 7, 8, 9, x} is 6.1, what is the value of x?

$$A = \frac{S}{n}$$

$$\frac{2 + 5 + 5 + 7 + 8 + 9 + x}{7} = \frac{36 + x}{7} = 6.1$$

Plug the given information into the average
formula, and solve for x.

$$36 + x = 6.1 \times 7$$
$$36 + x = 42.7$$
$$x = 6.7$$

In many average problems, only the SUM is important.

More complex average problems involve setting up two average formulas. For example:

Sam earned a $2,000 commission on a big sale, raising his average commission by $100. If Sam's new average commission is $900, how many sales has he made?

Before his big sale, Sam's average commission was $800:

$$A = \frac{S}{n} \rightarrow 800 = \frac{S}{n}$$

Before the sale: $S = 800n$

After his big sale, S went up by $2,000, n went up by 1, and the average was $900:

$$A = \frac{S}{n} \rightarrow 900 = \frac{S + 2000}{n + 1}$$

After the sale: $S + 2000 = 900(n + 1)$
$S + 2000 = 900n + 900$
$S + 1100 = 900n$

> To find the average of an evenly spaced set, simply take the middle number in the set.

Substituting $800n$ for S in the "after" equation allows us to solve for n:

$$S + 1100 = 900n$$
$$800n + 1100 = 900n$$
$$1100 = 100n$$
$$n = 11$$

Sam made 11 smaller sales before his big sale. Therefore, he made a total of 12 sales.

Evenly Spaced Sets: Take the Middle

You may recall that the average of a set of consecutive integers is the middle number. This is true for any set in which the terms are spaced evenly apart. For example:

The average of the set {3, 5, 7, 9, 11} is the middle term 7, because all the terms in the set are spaced evenly apart (in this case, they are spaced 2 units apart).

The average of the set {12, 20, 28, 36, 44, 52, 60, 68, 76} is the middle term 44, because all the terms in the set are spaced evenly apart (in this case, they are spaced 8 units apart).

Note that if an evenly spaced set has two "middle" numbers, the average of the set is the average of these two middle numbers. For example:

The average of the set {5, 10, 15, 20, 25, 30} is 17.5, because this is the average of the two middle numbers, 15 and 20.

You do not have to write out each term of an evenly spaced set to find the middle number—the average term. All you need to do to find the middle number is to add the first and last terms and divide that sum by 2. For example:

The average of the set {101, 111, 121 . . . 581, 591, 601} is equal to 351, which is the sum of the first and last terms (101 + 601 = 702) divided by 2 (702 ÷ 2 = 351).

*Manhattan*GMAT*Prep
the new standard

Median: The Middle Number

Some GMAT problems incorporate the concept of the median of a set. The median is the middle number of a set **that is ordered from least to greatest**. For example:

In the set {2, 3, 6, 6, 7, 8, 8, 8, 8, 8, 9}, the median is 8.
In the set {5, 17, 24, 25, 28}, the median is 24.

In sets with "two" middle numbers, the median is the average of these two middles:

In the set {3, 4, 9, 9}, the median is the average of 4 and 9, which is 6.5.
In the set {50, 51, 54, 58, 60, 62}, the median is the average of 54 and 58, which is 56.

For sets that include unknowns, a median can sometimes be determined even without knowing the value of the unknown. For example:

In the set {x, 2, 5, 11, 11, 12, 33}, the median is 11, irrespective of what x is. If x is less than 11, then 11 is the middle number. If x is more than 11, then 11 is the middle number. If x is equal to 11, then 11 is still the middle number.

However, in the set {x, x, 2, 4, 5}, the median cannot be determined without knowing the value of x. For example if $x = 1$, then the median is 2. But if $x = 5$, then the median is 5.

The GMAT often tests your knowledge of median in the context of an average problem. For example:

> **Given the ascending set {x, x, y, y, y, y}, what is greater, the median or the mean?**

Since we are told that the set is given to us in order, we know that the median is y.

We also know that the mean is the average of 4 y's and 2 x's.
Recall that $A = \dfrac{S}{n}$.   The sum of the numbers in the set is $4y + 2x$. The number of terms in the set, n, is 6.

When solving average problems, it is often more useful to deal with the sum of the terms than their average. If the mean, A, were greater than the median, the sum, S, would be greater than $6y$. So the question is really, is $4y + 2x$ less than $6y$? Since x is less than y, $4y + 2x$ is less than $6y$. Therefore, the mean must be less than y.

Given that the median is y, and the mean is less than y, in this set, the median is greater than the mean.

To find the median, list the numbers in the set from least to greatest, and take the middle number.

Standard Deviation

Standard deviation is a measure of how far data points in a distribution fall from the mean. Most GMAT problems that deal with standard deviation are fairly straightforward and do not require you to calculate standard deviation, only to apply it.

If the mean of a data set is 75 and the standard deviation is 10, what is the range of scores that fall within one standard deviation of the mean?

The range of scores that fall within one standard deviation is 65 - 85.

It is more important to understand what the standard deviation means than to learn how to calculate it.

A data set in which most of the points are close to the mean has a small standard deviation. A data set in which many of the points are scattered far from the mean has a larger standard deviation.

Large SD:	1, 7, 20, 50, 103
Small SD:	4, 6, 6, 7, 8, 8

To calculate the standard deviation of a set, subtract each term from the mean and square the differences. Then, average the squared differences and take the square root of this average. It is very unlikely that you will be asked to calculate a standard deviation on the GMAT. It is much more important that you know how to solve problems like the one above, and that you understand that standard deviation is a measure of how spread out a data set is. However, if you do need to calculate a standard deviation, you can do so according to the steps below:

Find the standard deviation of this set {3, 6, 8, 8, 10}.

(1) Find the mean of the set: $\dfrac{3 + 6 + 8 + 8 + 10}{5} = 7$

(2) Subtract each term from the mean, and square the differences:

$$7 - 3 = 4 \qquad\qquad 4^2 = 16$$
$$7 - 6 = 1 \qquad\qquad 1^2 = 1$$
$$7 - 8 = -1 \qquad\qquad (-1)^2 = 1$$
$$7 - 8 = -1 \qquad\qquad (-1)^2 = 1$$
$$7 - 10 = -3 \qquad\qquad (-3)^2 = 9$$

(3) Average the squared differences: $\dfrac{16 + 1 + 1 + 1 + 9}{5} = 5.6$

(4) Take the square root of 5.6 (the average): ≈ 2.37

Because this involves some complicated computation, it is unlikely that you will be asked to do this on the GMAT. However, seeing the steps involved in finding the standard deviation can help you to understand its meaning.

Problem Set

1. The average of 11 numbers is 10. When one number is eliminated, the average of the remaining numbers is 9.3. What is the eliminated number?

2. The average of 9, 11, and 16 is equal to the average of 21, 4.6, and what number?

3. Given the set of numbers {4, 5, 5, 6, 7, 8, 21}, how much higher is the mean than the median?

4. The sum of 8 numbers is 168. If one of the numbers is 28, what is the average of the other 7 numbers?

5. What is the average of the set of odd numbers {5, 7, 9, . . . 303, 305}?

6. If the average of the set {5, 6, 6, 8, 9, x, y} is 6, then what is the value of $x + y$?

7. There is a set of 160 numbers, beginning at 6, with each subsequent term increasing by an increment of 3. What is the average of this set of numbers?

8. A charitable association sold an average of 66 raffle tickets per member. Among the female members, the average was 70 raffle tickets. The male to female ratio of the association is 1:2. What was the average number of raffle tickets sold by the male members of the association?

9. On 4 sales, Matt received commissions of $300, $40, x, and $140. Without x, his average commission would be $50 lower. What is x?

10. The class mean score on a test was 60 and the standard deviation was 15. If Elena's score was within 2 standard deviations of the mean, what is the lowest score she could have received?

11. Matt gets a $1,000 commission on a big sale. This commission alone raises his average commission by $150. If Matt's new average commission is $400, how many sales has Matt made?

12. Matt starts a new job, with a goal of doubling his old average commission of $400. He takes a 10% commission, making commissions of $100, $200, $250, $700, and $1,000 on his first 5 sales. If Matt made two sales on the last day of the week, how much would Matt have had to sell in order to meet his goal?

13. There is a set of numbers in ascending order: {$y - x, y, y, y, y, x, x, x, x + y$}. If the mean is 9, and the median is 7, what is x?

Manhattan **GMAT** Prep
the new standard

14.   Grace's average bowling score over the past 6 games is 150. If she wants to raise her average score by 10%, and she has two games left in the season, what must her average score on the last two games be?

15.   If the average of x and y is 50, and the average of y and z is 80, what is the value of $z - x$?

the new standard

1. **17:** If the average of 11 numbers is 10, their sum is $11 \times 10 = 110$. After one number is eliminated, the average is 9.3, so the sum of the 10 remaining numbers is $10 \times 9.3 = 93$. The number eliminated is the difference between these sums: $110 - 93 = 17$.

2. **10.4:** $9 + 11 + 16 = 21 + 4.6 + x$
$$x = 10.4$$

3. **2:** The mean of the set is the sum of the numbers divided by the number of terms: $56 \div 7 = 8$. The median is the middle number: 6. 8 is 2 greater than 6.

4. **20:** The sum of the other 7 numbers is 140 $(168 - 28)$. So, the average of the numbers is:
$$\frac{140}{7} = 20$$

5. **155:** The average of an evenly spaced set is just the middle number, or the average of the first and last terms:
$$\frac{5 + 305}{2} = 155$$

6. **8:** If the average of 7 terms is 6, then the sum of the terms is 7×6, or 42. The listed terms have a sum of 34. Therefore, the remaining terms, x and y, must have a sum of $42 - 34$, or 8.

7. **244.5:** The average of an evenly spaced set is just the middle number, or the average of the first and last terms. The first term in this sequence is 6. The 160th term is $6 + (159 \times 3)$, or 483.
$$\frac{6 + 483}{2} = 244.5$$

8. **58:** There are x men and $2x$ women in the charity group. All in all, $3x$ people sold $3x \times 66$ raffle tickets, or $198x$ tickets. The $2x$ women in the group sold $2x \times 70$ raffle tickets, or $140x$ tickets. Therefore, the men sold $198x - 140x$ tickets, or $58x$ tickets. Since there are x men in the group, the average number of tickets sold by the male members of the group is $58x \div x$, or 58 tickets.

Alternately, you can set up two equations to solve this problem:
$$\frac{f(70) + mx}{m + f} = 66 \qquad \frac{m}{f} = \frac{1}{2}$$

Cross-multiply the second equation to yield the relationship $f = 2m$. Then, substitute this expression for f in the first equation:
$$\frac{2m(70) + mx}{3m} = 66$$
$$\frac{140 + x}{3} = 66$$
$$140 + x = 198$$
$$x = 58$$

9. **$360:** Without x, Matt's average sale is $(300 + 40 + 140) \div 3$, or $160. With x, Matt's average is $50 more, or $210. Therefore, the sum of $(300 + 40 + 140 + x) = 4(210) = 840$, and $x =$ $360.

10. **30:** Elena's score was within 2 standard deviations of the mean. Since the standard deviation is 15, her score is no more than 30 points from the mean. The lowest possible score she could have received, then, is $60 - 30$, or 30.

11. **5:** Before the $1,000 commission, Matt's average commission was $250; we can express this algebraically with the equation $S = 250n$.

After the sale, the sum of Matt's sales increased by $1,000, the number of sales made increased by 1, and his average commission was $400. We can express this algebraically with the equation:

$$S + 1000 = 400(n + 1)$$

Solve by substitution:

$$250n + 1000 = 400(n + 1)$$
$$250n + 1000 = 400n + 400$$
$$150n = 600$$
$$n = 4$$

Before the big sale, Matt had made 4 sales. Including the big sale, Matt has made 5 sales.

12. **$33,500:** On the first five sales, Matt earns a total of $2,250. In order for the average commission of 7 sales to be $800, the sum of those sales must be $7 \times \$800$, or $5,600.

$$A = \frac{S}{n} \quad \rightarrow \quad \frac{2250 + x}{7} = 800 \quad \rightarrow \quad 2250 + x = 5600$$

Therefore, Matt must earn an additional $5,600 - \$2,250$, or $3,350, in commissions. Matt's commission is 10%, so we can set up a proportion to calculate the total sales he needs to earn a commission of $3,350:

$$\frac{10}{100} = \frac{3350}{x}$$
$$x = \$33,500$$

13. **13:** The median number is the number in the middle of the set, or y. Therefore, $y = 7$. If the mean is 9, we can substitute numbers into the average formula as follows:

$$\frac{7 - x + 4(7) + 3x + x + 7}{9} = 9$$
$$3x + 42 = 81$$
$$3x = 39$$
$$x = 13$$

*Manhattan*GMAT*Prep
the new standard

14. **210:** Grace wants to raise her average score by 10%. Since 10% of 150 is 15, her target average is 165. Grace's total score is 150×6, or 900. If, in 8 games, she wants to have an average score of 165, then she will need a total score of 165×8, or 1,320. This is a difference of $1,320 - 900$, or 420. Her average score in the next two games must be: $420 \div 2 = 210$.

15. **60:** The sum of two numbers is twice their average. Therefore,

$$x + y = 100 \qquad\qquad y + z = 160.$$
$$x = 100 - y \qquad\qquad z = 160 - y$$

Substitute these expressions for z and x:

$$z - x = (160 - y) - (100 - y) = 160 - y - 100 + y = 160 - 100 = 60$$

Chapter 7
of
WORD TRANSLATIONS

OVERLAPPING
SETS

In This Chapter . . .

- The Double-Set Matrix
- Overlapping Sets and Percents
- Overlapping Sets and Algebraic Representation
- 3-Set Problems: Venn Diagrams

OVERLAPPING SETS

Translation problems which involve 2 or more given sets of data that partially intersect with each other are termed Overlapping Sets. For example:

> **30 people are in a room. 20 of them play golf. 15 of them play golf and tennis. If everyone plays at least one of the two sports, how many of the people play tennis only?**

This problem involves two sets: (1) people who play golf and (2) people who play tennis. The two sets overlap because some of the people who play golf also play tennis. Thus, these 2 sets can actually be divided into 4 categories:

(1)   People who only play golf   (3)   People who play golf and tennis
(2)   People who only play tennis   (4)   People who play neither sport

Solving double-set GMAT problems, like the example above, involves finding values for these four categories.

> *Use a double-set matrix to solve problems that involve overlapping sets.*

The Double-Set Matrix

GMAT problems that involve two sets can be solved by setting up a double-set matrix. This is the most efficient way of visualizing the four categories into which set members can be placed. For example:

> **Of 30 integers, 15 are in set A, 22 are in set B, and 8 are in both set A and B. How many of the integers are in NEITHER set A nor set B?**

This box shows the overlap.

	A	NOT A	TOTAL
B	8		22
NOT B			
TOTAL	15		30

This box shows the total members in SET A.

This box shows those members in NEITHER set.

This box shows the total members in SET B.

This box in the lower right corner is the key. This tells you how many distinct members exist in both of the sets.

Once the information given in the problem has been filled in, complete the chart, using the totals to guide you. (Each row and each column sum to a total value.)

	A	NOT A	TOTAL
B	8	14	22
NOT B	7	1	8
TOTAL	15	15	30

The question asks for the number of integers in neither set. We look at the chart and find the number of integers that are NOT A and NOT B; we find that the answer is 1.

Overlapping Sets and Percents

Complicated overlapping sets problems can involve percents. Don't be thrown by this! Continue to use the double-set matrix to organize the information given in the problem. Use the Smart Number, 100, to represent the total. For example, consider the problem below.

> **70% of the guests at Company X's annual holiday party are employees of Company X. 10% of the guests are women who are not employees of Company X. If half the guests at the party are men, what percent of the guests are female employees of Company X?**

First, fill in 100 for the total number of guests at the party. Then, fill in the other information given in the problem: 70% of the guests are employees, and 10% are women who are not employees. We also know that half the guests are men. (Therefore, we also know that half the guests are women.)

	Men	**Women**	**TOTAL**
Employee			70
Not Emp.		10	
TOTAL	50	50	100

Next, use subtraction to fill in the rest of the information in the matrix:
$100 - 70 = 30$ guests who are not employees
$30 - 10 = 20$ men who are not employees
$50 - 10 = 40$ female employees

	Men	**Women**	**TOTAL**
Employee	30	40	70
Not Emp.	20	10	30
TOTAL	50	50	100

40% of the guests at the party are female employees of Company X. Note that the problem does not require us to complete the matrix with the number of male employees, since we have already answered the question asked in the problem. However, completing the matrix is an excellent way to check your computation. The last box you fill in must work both vertically and horizontally.

Overlapping Sets and Algebraic Representation

When solving overlapping sets problems, it is imperative that you pay close attention to the wording of the problem. For example, consider the problem below:

> **Santa estimates that 10% of the children in the world have been good this year but don't celebrate Christmas, and that 50% of the children who celebrate Christmas have been good this year. If 40% of the children in the world have been good, what percentage of children in the world are not good and don't celebrate Christmas?**

Read the problem very carefully to determine whether you need to use algebra to represent unknowns.

WRONG

It is tempting to fill in the number 50 to represent the percent of good children who celebrate Christmas. However, this is incorrect.

	Good	Not Good	TOTAL
X-mas	50		
no X-mas	10		
TOTAL			100

CORRECT

Notice that, in this problem, we are told that 50% of the children *who celebrate Christmas* have been good. This is different from being told that 50% of the children in the world have been good. In this problem, this

	Good	Not Good	TOTAL
X-mas	.5x		x
no X-mas	10		
TOTAL	40		100

information we have is a fraction of an unknown number. We do not yet know how many children celebrate Christmas. Therefore, we cannot assign a number to represent the good children who celebrate Christmas. Instead, we represent the unknown total number of children who celebrate Christmas with the variable x, and the number of good children who celebrate Christmas with the expression .5x.

From the relationships in the table, we can set up an equation to solve for x.

$$.5x + 10 = 40$$
$$x = 60$$

	Good	Not Good	TOTAL
X-mas	.5x = 30	30	x = 60
no X-mas	10	30	40
TOTAL	40	60	100

With this information, we can fill in the rest of the table.

30% of the children are not good and don't celebrate Christmas.

3-Set Problems: Venn Diagrams

Problems that involve 3 overlapping sets can be solved by using a Venn Diagram.

> **Workers are grouped by their areas of expertise, and are placed on at least one team. 20 are on the Marketing team, 30 are on the Sales team, and 40 are on the Vision team. 5 workers are on both the Marketing and Sales teams, 6 workers are on both the Sales and Vision teams, 9 workers are on both the Marketing and Vision teams, and 4 workers are on all three teams. How many workers are there in total?**

In order to solve this problem, use a Venn Diagram. A Venn Diagram should be used ONLY for problems that involve three sets. Stick to the double-set matrix for two-set problems.

Work from the INSIDE OUT.

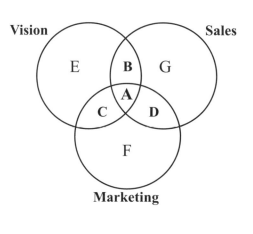

Begin your Venn Diagram by drawing three overlapping circles and labeling each one.

Notice that there are 7 different sections in a Venn Diagram. There is one innermost section **(A)** where all 3 circles overlap. This contains individuals who are on all 3 teams. There are three sections **(B, C, and D)** where 2 circles overlap. These contain individuals who are on 2 teams. There are three non-overlapping sections **(E, F, and G)** that contain individuals who are on only 1 team.

Venn Diagrams are easy to work with, if you remember one simple rule: **Work from the Inside Out.**

That is, it is easiest to begin by filling in a number in the innermost section **(A)**. Then, fill in numbers in the middle sections **(B, C, and D)**. Fill in the outermost sections **(E, F, and G)** last.

First: Workers on all 3 teams: Fill in the innermost circle. This is given in the problem as 4.

Second: Workers on 2 teams: Here we must remember to subtract those workers who are on all 3 teams. For example, the problem says that there are 5 workers on the Marketing and Sales teams. However, this includes the 4 workers who are on all three teams. Therefore, in order to deter-

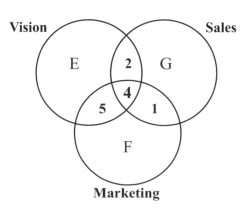

mine the number of workers who are on the Marketing and Sales teams exclusively, we must subtract the 4 workers who are on all three teams. We are left with $5 - 4 = 1$. The number of workers on the Marketing and Vision teams exclusively is $9 - 4 = 5$. The number of workers on the Sales and Vision teams exclusively is $6 - 4 = 2$.

Third: <u>Workers on 1 team only:</u> Here we must remember to subtract those workers who are on 2 teams and those workers who are on 3 teams. For example, the problem says that there are 20 workers on the Marketing team. But this includes the 1 worker who is on the Marketing and Sales teams, the 5 workers who are on the Marketing and Vision teams, and the 4 workers who are on all three teams. We must subtract all of these workers to find that there are $20 - 1 - 5 - 4 = 10$ people who are on the Marketing team exclusively. There are $30 - 1 - 2 - 4 = 23$ people on the Sales team exclusively. There are $40 - 2 - 5 - 4 = 29$ people on the Vision team exclusively.

In order to determine the total, just add all 7 numbers together = 74 total workers.

For 3-set problems, the GMAT usually specifies that everyone is on at least one team.

Problem Set

1. X and Y are sets of integers. X | Y denotes the set of integers that belong to set X or set Y, but not both. If X consists of 10 integers, Y consists of 18 integers, and 5 of the integers are in both X and Y, then X | Y consists of how many integers?

2. All of the members of Gym 1 live in Building A or Building B. There are 350 members of Gym 1. 200 people live in Building A across the street. 400 people live in Building B. 100 people from Building A are members of Gym 1. How many people live in Building B that do not belong to Gym 1?

3. Of 28 people in a park, 12 are children and the rest are adults. 8 people have to leave at 3 pm; the rest do not. If after 3 pm, there are 6 children still in the park, how many adults are still in the park?

4. Of 30 snakes at the reptile house, 10 have stripes, 21 are poisonous, and 5 have no stripes and are not poisonous. How many of the snakes have stripes AND are poisonous?

5. There are 30 stocks. 8 are volatile; the rest are blue-chip. 14 are tech; the rest are non-tech. If there are 3 volatile tech stocks, how many blue-chip non-tech stocks are there?

6. Students are in clubs as follows: Science - 20, Drama - 30, and Band - 12. No student is in all three clubs, but 8 are in both Science and Drama, 6 are in both Science and Band, and 4 are in Drama and Band. How many different students are in at least one of the three clubs?

7. 40% of all high school students hate roller coasters; the rest love them. 20% of those students who love roller coasters own chinchillas. What percentage of students love roller coasters but do not own a chinchilla?

8. There are 26 students who have read a total of 56 books among them. The only books they have read, though, are Aye, Bee, Cod, and Dee. If 10 students have only read Aye, and 8 students have read only Cod and Dee, what is the smallest number of books any of the remaining students could have read?

9. Scout candies come in red, white, or blue. They can also be hard or soft. There are 50 candies: 20 red, 20 white, and 10 blue. There are 25 hard and 25 soft. If there are 5 soft blue candies and 12 soft red candies, how many hard white candies are there?

10. Of 60 children, 30 are happy, 10 are sad, and 20 are neither happy nor sad. There are 20 boys and 40 girls. If there are 6 happy boys and 4 sad girls, how many boys are neither happy nor sad?

11.   10% of all aliens are capable of intelligent thought and have more than 3 arms, and 75% of aliens with 3 arms or less are capable of intelligent thought. If 40% of all aliens are capable of intelligent thought, what percent of aliens have more than 3 arms?

12.   There are three country clubs in town: Abacus, Bradley, and Claymore. Abacus has 300 members, Bradley 400, and Claymore has 450. 30 people belong to both Abacus and Bradley, 40 to both Abacus and Claymore, and 50 to both Bradley and Claymore. 20 people are members of all three clubs. How many people belong to at least 1 country club in town?

13.   There are 58 vehicles in a parking lot. 24 are trucks, 30 are cars, and the rest are some other vehicle. 20 of the vehicles are red, 16 are blue, and the rest are some other color. If there are 12 red trucks in the parking lot, 5 blue trucks, and 4 red cars, what is the largest possible number of blue cars in the parking lot?

14.   The 38 movies in the video store fall into the following three categories: 10 action, 20 drama, and 18 comedy. However, some movies are classified under more than one category: 5 are both action and drama, 3 are both action and comedy, and 4 are both drama and comedy. How many action - drama - comedies are there?

15.   There are 6 stores in town that had a total of 20 visitors on a particular day. However, only 10 people went shopping that day; some people visited more than one store. If 6 people visited exactly two stores each, and everyone visited at least one store, what is the largest number of stores anyone could have visited?

1. **18:** Use a Double-Set Matrix to solve this problem. First, fill in the numbers given in the problem: There are 10 integers in set X and 18 integers in set Y. There are 5 integers that are in both sets. Then, use subtraction to figure out that there are 5 integers that are in set X and not in set Y, and 13 integers that are in set Y and not in set X. This is all the information you need to solve this problem: X | Y = 5 + 13 = 18.

	Set X	NOT Set X	TOTAL
Set Y	5	13	18
NOT Set Y	5		
TOTAL	10		

2. **150:** Use a Double-Set Matrix to solve this problem. First, fill in the numbers given in the problem: 350 people who belong to the gym, 200 people who live in Building A, 400 people who live in Building B, and 100 gym members from Building A. Then, use subtraction to figure out that there are 250 people from Building B who belong to the gym and 150 people from Building B who do not belong to the gym.

	Building A	Building B	TOTAL
Gym	100	250	350
NOT Gym		150	
TOTAL	200	400	

3. **14:** Use a Double-Set Matrix to solve this problem. First, fill in the numbers given in the problem: 28 total people in the park, 12 children and the rest (16) adults; 8 leave at 3 pm and the rest (20) stay. Then, we are told that there are 6 children left in the park after 3pm. Since we know there are a total of 20 people in the park after 3pm, the remaining 14 people must be adults.

	Children	Adults	TOTAL
Leave at 3			8
Stay	6	14	20
TOTAL	12	16	28

4. **6:** Use a Double-Set Matrix to solve this problem. First, fill in the numbers given in the problem: 30 snakes, 10 with stripes (and therefore 20 without), 21 that are poisonous (and therefore 9 that aren't), and 5 that are neither striped nor poisonous. Use subtraction to fill in the rest of the chart. 6 snakes have stripes and are poisonous.

	Stripes	No Stripes	TOTAL
Poisonous	6		21
Not Poison.	4	5	9
TOTAL	10	20	30

5. **11:** Use a Double-Set Matrix to solve this problem. First, fill in the numbers given in the problem: There are 30 stocks. 8 are volatile; the rest are blue-chip. 14 are tech; the rest are non-tech. We also know that there are 3 volatile tech stocks. Therefore, by subtraction, there are 5 volatile non-tech stocks, and there are 11 blue-chip non-tech stocks.

	Volatile	Blue-Chip	TOTAL
Tech	3		14
Non-Tech	5	11	16
TOTAL	8	22	30

*Manhattan*GMAT*Prep

6. **44:** There are three overlapping sets here; therefore, use a Venn diagram to solve the problem. First, fill in the numbers given in the problem, working from the inside out: no students in all three clubs, 8 in Science and Drama, 6 in Science and Band, and 4 in Drama and Band. Then, use the totals for each club to determine how many students are in only one club. For example, we know that there are 30 students in the Drama club. So far, we have placed 12 students in the circle that represents the Drama club (8 who are in Science and Drama, and 4 who are in Band and Drama). $30 - 12 = 18$, the number of students who are in only the Drama Club. Use this process to determine the number of students in just the Science and Band clubs as well. To find the number of students in at least one of the clubs, sum all the numbers in the diagram:
$6 + 18 + 2 + 6 + 8 + 4 = 44$.

7. **48:** Since all the numbers in this problem are given in percentages, assign a grand total of 100 students. We know that 40% of all high school students hate roller coasters, so we fill in 40 for this total and 60 for the number of students who love roller coasters. We also

	Love R.C.	Don't	TOTAL
Chinchilla	12		
No Chinch.	48		
TOTAL	60	40	100

know that 20% **of those students who love roller coasters** own chinchillas. It does not say that 20% of all students own chinchillas. Since 60% of students love roller coasters, 20% of 60% own chinchillas. Therefore, we fill in 12 for the students who both love roller coasters and own chinchillas. The other 48 roller coaster lovers do not own chinchillas.

8. **2:** According to the problem, 10 students have read only 1 book: Aye, and 8 students have read 2 books: Cod and Dee. This accounts for 18 students, who have read a total of 26 books among them. Therefore, there are 8 students left to whom we can assign books, and there are 30 books left to assign. We can assume that one of these 8 students will have read the smallest possible number if the other 7 have read the maximum number: all 4 books. If 7 students have read 4 books each, this accounts for another 28 books, leaving only 2 for the eighth student to have read. Note

Students	Books Read
10	10
8	16
7	28
1	2
26	56

that it is impossible for the eighth student to have read only one book. If we assign one of the students to have read only 1 book, this leaves 29 books for 7 students. This is slightly more than 4 books per students. However, we know that there are only four books available; it is therefore impossible for one student to have read more than four books.

9. **12:** Use a Double-Set Matrix to solve this problem, with the "color" set divided into 3 categories instead of only 2. First, fill in the numbers given in the problem: 20 red, 20 white, and 10 blue, 25 hard and 25 soft. We also know there are 5 soft blue candies and 12 soft red

	Red	White	Blue	TOTAL
Hard		12		25
Soft	12	8	5	25
TOTAL	20	20	10	50

candies. Therefore, by subtraction, there are 8 soft white candies, and there are 12 hard white candies.

10. **8:** Use a Double-Set Matrix to solve this problem, with the "mood" set divided into 3 categories instead of only 2. First, fill in the numbers given in the problem: of 60 children, 30 are happy, 10 are sad, and 20 are neither happy nor sad; 20 are boys and 40 are girls. We also know

	Happy	Sad	Neither	TOTAL
Boys	6	6	8	20
Girls		4		40
TOTAL	30	10	20	60

there are 6 happy boys and 4 sad girls. Therefore, by subtraction, there are 6 sad boys and there are 8 boys who are neither happy nor sad.

11. **60%:** Since all the numbers in this problem are given in percentages, assign a grand total of 100 aliens. We know that 10% of all aliens are capable of intelligent thought and have more than 3 arms. We also know that 75% **of aliens with 3 arms or less** are

	Thought	No Thought	TOTAL
> 3 arms	10		$100 - x$
≤ 3 arms	$.75x$		x
TOTAL	40		100

capable of intelligent thought. It does not say that 75% of all aliens are capable of intelligent thought. Therefore, assign the variable x to represent the percentage of aliens with three arms or less. Then, the percentage of aliens with three arms or less who are capable of intelligent thought can be represented by $.75x$. Since we know that 40% of all aliens are capable of intelligent thought, we can write the equation $10 + .75x = 40$, or $.75x = 30$. Solve for x: $x = 40$. Therefore, 40% of the aliens have three arms or less, and 60% of aliens have more than three arms.

12. **1050:** There are three overlapping sets here; therefore, use a Venn diagram to solve the problem. First, fill in the numbers given in the problem, working from the inside out. We know that 20 people are in all three clubs. If 30 people are in both A & B, then 10 are in A & B, but not C. If 40 people are in both A & C, then 20 are in A & C, but not B. If 50 people are in both B & C, then 30 are in B & C, but not A. Then, use the totals for each club to determine how many students are in only one club. For example, we know that Abacus has 300 members. So far, we have placed 50 people in the circle that represents Abacus (10 who are in A and B, 20 who are in A and C, and 20 who are in all three clubs). 300 − 50 = 250, the number of people who are in only the Abacus club.

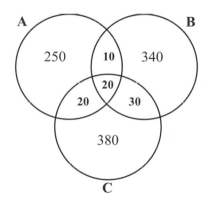

Use this process to determine the number of students in just the Bradley and Claymore clubs as well. To find the number of people in at least one of the clubs, sum all the numbers in the diagram: 250 + 340 + 380 + 10 + 20 + 30 + 20 = 1050.

13. **11:** Use a Double-Set Matrix to solve this problem. First, fill in the numbers given in the problem: 58 vehicles are in a parking lot. 24 are trucks, 30 are cars, and the rest some other vehicle. 20 of the vehicles are red, 16 are blue, and the rest are some other color. We also know there are 12 red trucks, 5 blue trucks, and 4 red cars. The

	Trucks	Cars	Other	TOTAL
Red	12	4	4	20
Blue	5		0	16
Other	7			22
TOTAL	24	30	4	58

critical total in this problem is that there are 16 blue vehicles. Since 5 of them are blue trucks, and (by filling in the matrix we see that) there are 0 "other" blue vehicles, there must be 11 blue cars in the lot.

14. **2:** There are three overlapping sets here; therefore, use a Venn diagram to solve the problem. First, fill in the numbers given in the problem, working from the inside out. Assign the variable x to represent the number of action - drama - comedies. Then, create variable expressions, using the totals given in the problem, to represent the number of movies in each of the other categories. We know that there is a total of 38 movies; therefore, we can write the following equation to represent the total number of movies in the store:

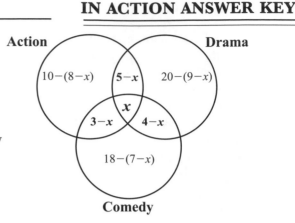

$$10 - 8 + x$$
$$20 - 9 + x$$
$$18 - 7 + x$$
$$5 - x$$
$$4 - x$$
$$3 - x$$
$$+ \qquad x$$
$$\overline{36 + x = 38}$$
$$x = 2$$

If you are unsure of the algebraic solution, you can also guess a number for x and fill in the rest of the diagram until the total number of movies reaches 38.

15. **5:** If 6 people visited exactly 2 stores each, this accounts for 12 of the visitors counted in the total. This leaves 4 people to account for the remaining 8 visitors. In order to assign the maximum number of stores to any one person, assign the minimum to the first three of the remaining people: 1 store. This leaves 5 stores for the fourth person to visit.

People	Store Visits
6	12
3	3
1	5
10	20

Chapter 8
of
WORD TRANSLATIONS

STRATEGIES FOR
DATA SUFFICIENCY

In This Chapter . . .

- Rephrasing: Translating Words into Algebra
- Sample Rephrasings for Challenging Problems

Rephrasing: Translating Words into Algebra

To solve word translation data sufficiency problems, you need to rephrase words into algebra. Any time you see a word problem in data sufficiency, you should immediately rephrase the information provided both in the question and in the statements. Be sure to keep track of the variables you assign to represent each unknown value. For example:

> **A hot dog vendor who sells only hot dogs and soft drinks charges $3 for a hot dog. If the vendor collected $1000 in total revenue last month, how much does he charge for soft drinks?**
>
> **(1) The vendor sold twice as many hot dogs as soft drinks last month.**
> **(2) The revenue from hot dog sales last month was 3/4 of the total monthly revenue.**

A   Statement (1) ALONE is sufficient, but statement (2) alone is not sufficient.
B   Statement (2) ALONE is sufficient, but statement (1) alone is not sufficient.
C   BOTH statements TOGETHER are sufficient, but NEITHER statement ALONE is sufficient.
D   EACH statement ALONE is sufficient.
E   Statements (1) and (2) together are NOT sufficient.

Be sure to make a note of what each variable represents.

First, assign variables and rephrase the information contained in the question itself by translating the words into algebraic equations:

> Let H = the number of hot dogs sold
> Let S = the number of soft drinks sold
> Let x = the price of soft drinks

The question can be rephrased as follows: **Given that $3H + xS = 1000$, what is x?**

Statement (1) can be rephrased as $H = 2S$. This allows us to substitute $2S$ in for H in the original equation.

$$3H + xS = 1000 \;\rightarrow\; 3(2S) + xS = 1000 \;\rightarrow\; 6S + xS = 1000$$

However, this still leaves us with 2 unknown variables. It is impossible to find the value of x without knowing the value of S. Thus, statement (1) alone is not sufficient to answer the question.

Statement (2) can be rephrased as $3H = 750$ or $H = 250$. We can substitute 250 for H in the original equation as follows:

$$3H + xS = 1000 \;\rightarrow\; 3(250) + xS = 1000 \;\rightarrow\; 750 + xS = 1000 \;\rightarrow\; xS = 250$$

However, without knowing the value of S, this is insufficient to find the variable x. Thus, statement (2) alone is not sufficient to answer the question.

If you combine the information given in both statements, you have two different equations with two unknown variables. Using substitution, you can solve for both S and x. Thus, the answer to this data sufficiency problem is (C): BOTH statements TOGETHER are sufficient, but NEITHER statement ALONE is sufficient.

Consider this example:

> **If the price of a gallon of milk and a loaf of bread both increased by 10% from 1987 to 1990, what was the price of a loaf of bread in 1987?**
>
> **(1) Together, a loaf of bread and a gallon of milk cost $3.60 in 1987.**
> **(2) Together, a loaf of bread and a gallon of milk cost $3.96 in 1990.**

First, assign variables and rephrase the information contained in the question itself.

> Let B = the price of a loaf of bread in 1987
> Let M = the price of a gallon of milk in 1987

The question can be rephrased as follows: **What is B?**

Statement (1) can be rephrased as $B + M = 3.60$. It is impossible to find the value of B without knowing the value of M. Picking extreme numbers illustrates this. The loaf of bread could have cost $3.55 and the gallon of milk $0.05. Or the reverse could have been true. Thus, statement (1) alone is NOT sufficient to answer the question.

Statement (2) can be rephrased as $1.1B + 1.1M = 3.96$. We are representing the price of a loaf of bread in 1990 as $1.1B$ because the question tells us that the price of a loaf of bread in 1990 was 10% greater than the price of a loaf of bread in 1987. The same logic holds for the price of a gallon of milk.

Notice that statement (2) can be rephrased further by dividing both sides of the equation by 1.1. This yields the following: $B + M = 3.60$. This is the same information as provided in statement (1)! As such, using the same logic as with statement (1), it is impossible to find the value of B without knowing the value of M. Thus, statement (2) alone is NOT sufficient to answer the question.

Looking at both statements together does not add any new information, since statement (2) provides the exact same information as statement (1).

The answer to this data sufficiency problem is (E): Statements (1) and (2) TOGETHER are NOT sufficient.

*Manhattan*GMAT*Prep
the new standard

Remember that you can often rephrase both the question *and* the statements.

Rephrasing: Challenge Short Set

At the very end of this book, you will find lists of WORD TRANSLATIONS problems that have appeared on past official GMAT exams. These lists reference problems from *The Official Guide for GMAT Review, 11th Edition* and *The Official Guide for GMAT Quantitative Review* (the questions contained therein are the property of The Graduate Management Admission Council, which is not affiliated in any way with Manhattan GMAT).

As you work through the Data Sufficiency problems listed at the end of this book, be sure to focus on *rephrasing*. If possible, try to *rephrase* each question into its simplest form *before* looking at the two statements. In order to rephrase, focus on figuring out the specific information that is absolutely necessary to answer the question. After rephrasing the question, you should also try to *rephrase* each of the two statements, if possible. Rephrase each statement by simplifying the given information into its most basic form.

In order to help you practice rephrasing, we have taken the most difficult Data Sufficiency problems on *The Official Guide* problem list (these are the problem numbers listed in the "Challenge Short Set" on page 123) and have provided you with our own sample rephrasings for each question and statement. In order to evaluate how effectively you are using the rephrasing strategy, you can compare your rephrased questions and statements to our own rephrasings that appear below. Questions and statements that are significantly rephrased appear in **bold**.

Rephrasings from *The Official Guide For GMAT Review, 11th Edition*

The questions and statements that appear below are only our *rephrasings*. The original questions and statements can be found by referencing the problem numbers below in the Data Sufficiency section of *The Official Guide for GMAT Review, 11th edition* (pages 278-290).

<u>Note</u>: Problem numbers preceded by "D" refer to questions in the Diagnostic Test chapter of *The Official Guide for GMAT Review, 11th edition* (pages 24-25).

D27. Let f = charge for the first minute
      Let a = number of additional minutes (after the first minute)
      Let r = rate for each additional minute
      Let T = total cost for the call

$T = f + a(r)$

What is $a + 1$?   OR   What is a?

(1) $T = 6.50$

(2) $T = f + a(r)$
    $T = (r + .50) + a(r)$

D29. The question itself cannot be rephrased. However, each statement can be rephrased using a double-set matrix as follows:

(1)

	Bought Business Computers	Did NOT Buy Business Computers	TOTAL
Own Store	$.85x$	$.15x$	x
Do NOT Own Store			
TOTAL	?		100

(2)

	Bought Business Computers	Did NOT Buy Business Computers	TOTAL
Own Store			40
Do NOT Own Store			60
TOTAL	?		100

D46.   Average salary last year for 10 employees = $42,800
Total salary paid to these 10 employees last year = $42,800(10) = $428,000

To find the average salary for these 10 employees this year:
What is the TOTAL amount paid to these 10 employees this year?

(1) Total paid to 8 employees THIS year = 1.15 × (Total paid to *these* 8 employees LAST year)
We do not know the total paid to *these* 8 employees last year, so we cannot calculate this year's total.

(2) Total paid to 2 employees THIS year = Total paid to *these* 2 employees LAST year
We do not know the total paid to *these* 2 employees last year, so we cannot calculate this year's total.

68. $A = \dfrac{j + k}{2}$

What is the value of $j + k$?

(1) $\dfrac{j + 2 + k + 4}{2} = 11$

$j + k = 16$

(2) $\dfrac{j + k + 14}{3} = 10$

$j + k = 16$

79. T = hours of additional travel time (the same for Cars X and Y)
R_x = rate of car X R_y = rate of car Y
$(T)R_x$ = distance of car X $(T)R_y$ = distance of car Y

For car X to increase its lead by 1 mile over car Y:
$(T)R_x = (T)R_y + 1$ which simplifies to $T(R_x - R_y) = 1$

What is the value of T ?   OR   What is the value of $R_x - R_y$?

(1) $R_x - R_y = 50 - 40 = 10$

(2) In 3/60 of an hour, car X increased its lead by 1/2 mile:
$(3/60)R_x = (3/60)R_y + 1/2$
$R_x - R_y = 10$

82.   Let x = the probability that the chip will be red
        Let y = the probability that the chip will be blue
        Let z = the probability that the chip will be white

        $x + y + z = 1$
        $y + z = 1 - x$

        What is the value of $(y + z)$? OR What is the value of $1 - x$?

        (1) $y = \dfrac{1}{5}$

        (2) $x = \dfrac{1}{3}$

94.   Let x = the number of student who DO study Spanish
        Let y = the number of students who do NOT study Spanish

	French	No French	TOTAL
Spanish	?	100	x
No Spanish		0	y
TOTAL	200	100	300

        What is the value of x or y?

        (1) $y = 60$

        (2) $x = 240$

120.   In order to average 120 or more words per paragraph, the report would need to contain at least $25(120) = 3000$ total words.

        The first 23 paragraphs of the report contain 2600 total words.

        Does the 2-paragraph preface contain fewer than 400 words?

        (1) The 2-paragraph preface contains more than 200 words.

        (2) The 2-paragraph preface contains fewer than 300 words.

155.   Let c = the capacity of the bucket

What is the value of c?

(1) Let x = the amount of water in the bucket
    $x = 9$

(2) $3 + 1/2c = 4/3(1/2c)$

Rephrasings from *The Official Guide for GMAT Quantitative Review*

The questions and statements that appear below are only our *rephrasings*. The original questions and statements can be found by referencing the problem numbers below in the Data Sufficiency section of *The Official Guide for GMAT Quantitative Review* (pages 149-157).

29.   Let c = the number of questions John answered correctly on the test

What is the value of c?

(1) Let f = the number of questions John answered correctly out of the first 30 questions
Let s = the number of questions John answered correctly out of the second 30 questions
$f = 7 + s$
$f + s = c$

(2) $c = 5/6(30) + 4/5(30)$

38.   Let x = rate of machine X
Let y = rate of machine Y

Machine X produces 100 cans in 2 hours. Therefore, $x = 50$.

What is $x + y$?   **OR**   **What is y?**

(1) $x = y$

(2) $x + y = 2x$

50.   **Can all of these variables be expressed in terms of one of the variables?**

(1) $z = 1$ AND $y = 32/x$

(2) $x = 2y$ AND $y = 4z$
$x = 2(4z) = 8z$

the new standard

65.   Let c = the number of cars produced
       Let t = the number of trucks produced

       What is the ratio of $\dfrac{c}{t}$?

       (1) $1.08c = 1.5t$

       $$\frac{c}{t} = \frac{1.5}{1.08}$$

       (2) $\dfrac{c}{t} = \dfrac{565,000}{406,800}$

71.   **Does $z = 18$?**

       (1) $x + y + z = 18$

       (2) $x = -y$

99. $0 < x < 10$

       Is $z > \dfrac{x + 10}{2}$?

       (1) No rephrasing is possible. Test different values for z and x.

       (2) $z = 5x$

107.   Testing numbers is the easiest way to solve this problem.

112. x is an integer.
       Is y an integer?

       (1) $x + y + y - 2 = 3x$
           $y = x + 1$

       (2) 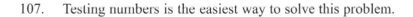 $\dfrac{x + y}{2}$ = not an integer. Test numbers to prove this information insufficient.

Chapter 9
of
WORD TRANSLATIONS

OFFICIAL GUIDE
PROBLEM SETS

In This Chapter . . .

- Word Translations Problem Solving List
  from *The Official Guides*
- Word Translations Data Sufficiency List
  from *The Official Guides*

Practicing with REAL GMAT Problems

Now that you have completed your study of WORD TRANSLATIONS it is time to test your skills on problems that have actually appeared on real GMAT exams over the past several years.

The problem sets that follow are composed of questions from two books published by the Graduate Management Admission Council® (the organization that develops the official GMAT exam):

The Official Guide for GMAT Review, 11th Edition &
The Official Guide for GMAT Quantitative Review

These two books contain quantitative questions that have appeared on past official GMAT exams. (The questions contained therein are the property of The Graduate Management Admission Council, which is not affiliated in any way with Manhattan GMAT.)

Although the questions in the Official Guides have been "retired" (they will not appear on future official GMAT exams), they are great practice questions.

In order to help you practice effectively, we have categorized every problem in The Official Guides by topic and subtopic. On the following pages, you will find two categorized lists:

(1) **Problem Solving:** Lists all Problem Solving WORD TRANSLATION questions contained in *The Official Guides* and categorizes them by subtopic.

(2) **Data Sufficiency:** Lists all Data Sufficiency WORD TRANSLATION questions contained in *The Official Guides* and categorizes them by subtopic.

Note: Each book in Manhattan GMAT's 8-book preparation series contains its own *Official Guide* lists that pertain to the specific topic of that particular book. If you complete all the practice problems contained on the *Official Guide* lists in the back of each of the 8 Manhattan GMAT preparation books, you will have completed every single question published in *The Official Guides*. At that point, you should be ready to take your Official GMAT exam!

Problem Solving

from *The Official Guide for GMAT Review, 11th edition* (pages 20-23 & 152-186) and *The Official Guide for GMAT Quantitative Review* (pages 62-85)

Note: Problem numbers preceded by "D" refer to questions in the Diagnostic Test chapter of *The Official Guide for GMAT Review, 11th edition* (pages 20-23).

Solve each of the following problems in a notebook, making sure to demonstrate how you arrived at each answer by showing all of your work and computations. If you get stuck on a problem, look back at the WORD TRANSLATIONS strategies and content contained in this guide to assist you.

CHALLENGE SHORT SET

This set contains the more difficult word translation problems from each of the content areas.

> *11th edition*: D6, D14, 64, 87, 170, 182, 193, 200, 208, 212, 217, 218, 223, 224, 239
> *Quantitative Review*: 23, 87, 119, 129, 130

FULL PROBLEM SET

Algebraic Translations

> *11th edition*: 24, 47, 74, 91, 92, 140, 153, 200, 210
> *Quantitative Review*: 17, 23, 62, 76, 127, 131

Rates and Work

> *11th edition*: 19, 25, 82, 87, 103, 126, 154, 185, 223
> *Quantitative Review*: 14, 20, 21, 35, 87, 90, 119, 130, 136, 140

Ratios

> *11th edition*: 18, 50, 52, 61, 63, 73, 76, 97, 106, 118, 163, 168, 170, 181, 193, 196
> *Quantitative Review*: 71, 82

Combinatorics & Probability

> *11th edition*: D7, 10, 64, 121, 135, 173, 195, 217, 231
> *Quantitative Review*: 80, 132, 151

Statistics

> *11th edition*: D9, 11, 54, 65, 68, 93, 101, 119, 132, 149, 182, 186, 203, 208, 212, 218, 224
> *Quantitative Review*: 30, 59, 63, 70, 84, 129, 137, 148, 157, 161

Overlapping Sets

> *11th edition*: D4, D6, D14, 79, 169, 166, 179, 214, 239
> *Quantitative Review*: 16

Miscellaneous (Graphs, Computation, and Non-Standard Problems)

Solve by charting, listing, drawing pictures, and employing logical reasoning.

> *11th edition*: 1, 27, 32, 72, 88, 95, 116, 141
> *Quantitative Review*: 49, 50, 54, 94, 105, 110, 126, 168

*Manhattan*GMAT*Prep
the new standard

Data Sufficiency

from *The Official Guide for GMAT Review, 11th edition* (pages 24-25 & 278-290) and *The Official Guide for GMAT Quantitative Review* (pages 149-157).

Note: Problem numbers preceded by "D" refer to questions in the Diagnostic Test chapter of *The Official Guide for GMAT Review, 11th edition* (pages 24-25).

Solve each of the following problems in a notebook, making sure to demonstrate how you arrived at each answer by showing all of your work. If you get stuck on a problem, look back at the WORD TRANSLATIONS strategies and content contained in this guide to assist you.

Practice REPHRASING both the questions and the statements. The majority of data sufficiency problems can be rephrased; however, if you have difficulty rephrasing a problem, try testing numbers to solve it.

CHALLENGE SHORT SET

This set contains the more difficult word translation problems from each of the content areas.

> *11th edition*: D27, D29, D46, 68, 79, 82, 94, 120, 155
> *Quantitative Review*: 29, 38, 50, 65, 71, 99, 107, 112

FULL PROBLEM SET

Algebraic Translations

> *11th edition*: D27, 53, 73, 92, 98, 100, 115, 155
> *Quantitative Review*: 12, 17, 26, 27, 29, 81, 93, 104

Rates and Work

> *11th edition*: 19, 33, 63, 79, 81, 93
> *Quantitative Review*: 38, 47, 54, 69

Ratios

> *11th edition*: 2, 95, 130, 138
> *Quantitative Review*: 11, 24, 31, 50, 65, 74

Combinatorics & Probability

> *11th edition*: 10, 82

Statistics

> *11th edition*: D31, D32, D43, D46, 68, 104, 114, 120, 141
> *Quantitative Review*: 34, 41, 71, 97, 99, 107, 112

Overlapping Sets

> *11th edition*: D29, D34, D47, 49, 90, 94
> *Quantitative Review*: 10, 62

Miscellaneous (Graphs, Computation, and Non-Standard Problems)

> *11th edition*: D45, 13, 36, 44, 71, 87, 88, 96, 106
> *Quantitative Review*: 8